NEVER STOP DANCING

NEVER STOP DANCING

RALPH G. MARTELL

Pan Publications
P.O. Box 231
Bouckville, New York

Never Stop Dancing

Jacket Design/Concept
by
Ralph G. Martell

Graphics and Book Design
by
John D. Mahaffy

ISBN 0-9634828-2-3

Published by
Pan Publications
P.O. Box 231
Bouckville, New York 13310

Dedication

To all those struggling and would-be writers that hope to see their words in print.

True, it's vainglory and we're puffed up for a moment, like a child's iridescent and ephemeral soap bubble that for a moment mesmerizes us - then poof it's gone! We are bewildered for a second, but then others are blown and we forget.

To my son Nevin and daughter Josephine, who I hope will ride the wind of change into a world of tolerance and love.

Forword

Forget the potholes behind you. Watch out for the ones ahead.

Time has a way of ignoring us and marching on. If we don't get in step, it walks over us.

It has been two years since my last book and I do feel slightly trampled on, but none the worse for wear. I see light at the end of the tunnel (I hope it isn't my house burning!)

Contents

Prose & Poetry

Half Witicisms

Wanderings

The Cuban Constellation

Again *Américas* magazine, published by OAS, the Organization of American States, in its January/February 1995 issue invoked a predestined call for me to travel.

Because of an article on Uruguay in the March/April 1994 issue, I was lured to Uruguay and was invited to write for their tourist board. This time it was Cuba, a place I had not visited in forty-five years, when I went as a young romantic with raging hormones.

The Cuba article featured the Caribbean Music and Dance Program. The trip was designed mainly for serious musicians with a strong interest in the study of Afro/Cuban rhythms and social dancers eager to make a Latin connection.

Although I was neither, I have always had a great passion for Latin music, especially Afro/Cuban jazz, so I thought this would be the perfect vehicle for my gaining permission to travel to Cuba.

I wrote to the Caribbean Music and Dance Program and sent them one of my books and numerous writeups. One of the principles, Lisa Maria Salb, phoned me (She is also a fluent translator, dancer and singer.) and invited me to join the group. She said a visa could be arranged for me as a journalist. Subsequently I heard from Deborah Rubenstein and Melissa Daar, both dancers, and co-founders of the Caribbean Music and Dance Program.

My local New York newspaper, the *Clinton Courier*, gave me a letter of assignment and the South American Explorers Club in Ithaca, New York, of which I am a member, expressed an interest in an article for their magazine.

The ice was thinning after a bizarre late January thaw, and the thought of more ice fishing began to lose its appeal as I looked out over my semi-frozen pond from my cabin windows on Leland Pond.

There was plenty of time for preparation, but each purchase of some small article seemed to hasten the departure date.

My friend Richard, who owns a thriving construction business, expressed an interest in seeing Cuba, but the last minute death of a friend out in Oregon and lucrative contracts and bids enticed him to stay at home and fill his coffers.

There was constant contact from the Caribbean Music and Dance Programs and they sent me all kinds of literature and travel advisories. They were dependable, friendly and efficient. Their address is: 37 Dearborn St., San Francisco, CA 94110. Telephone (415) 861-7107. They have several workshops throughout the year.

As it turned out my departure date was Feb. 9, 1995, my sixty-eighth birthday, and I felt in the prime of my youth (well, almost), in my head and spirit, certainly.

Anticipation is one of the great rewards of traveling. I had read everything available on Cuba and I knew not to expect the glory and gaiety of Old Havana, but I could not resist referring to my youthful memories.

The great day arrived. My bold-faced alarm gave off a digital staccato bleat and I thrust my legs out onto the cold floors so there would be no chance of falling back asleep.

Soon I was dressed and out the door, into a cold black morning without the aid of coffee. I took the car out of a warm garage and drove it to the cottage door, then struggled with my suitcase through mounds of snow, vapor pouring out of my nostrils like some embattled dragon.

The night before I had called my daughter, Josephine, and son, Nevin, at their respective schools, and gave them emergency numbers in Havana. Josephine wanted to jump ship and come with me.

My destination was Nassau, in the Bahamas, where I had worked as a bartender at the British Colonial Hotel as a bartender around 1949. It was all so strange.

After a change in Charlotte, North Carolina, which was enduring below freezing temperatures, off we went into the wild blue yonder. Only then did I remember that it was my birthday; I ignored the passed years.

Soon we were looking down on a turquoise ocean and coral reefs, which quickly revived me. On arrival it was cool, dry and pleasant for me, but cold for the Bahamians. I took a taxi to the Towne Hotel, my arranged stayover. It was pink and plain, the employees all genuinely courteous and happy. I was shown to a clean and simply furnished room; I was content.

In the lobby I met Pat, part of our group, writing postcards. Her enthusiasm overwhelms you but you know it's "real" and you cannot resist her. After an introduction we agreed on a walk with John, a jazz flute player, who had been sleeping off his jet lag from California.

Eager to see my alma mater, I headed for the British Colonial Hotel just a few blocks away. It dominated the small downtown area, a huge sprawling faded pink stucco giant with turrets built at the turn of the century. It had been refurbished, and so had my memory. I could not associate reality with nostalgia.

Tourists were as common as ants, except they had bulging wallets and a determined shoppers' gleam in their eyes. The back streets were still colorful and had many of the old charming clapboard buildings that I remembered, with verandahs and shuttered windows.

At the post office I met some friendly Bahamians celebrating "The Tricentenary of Nassau.

Later I hooked up with Pat and John and we went to Paradise Island, where you had to pay a toll. It was like Disneyland, filled with massive hotels. I recoiled in disgust, remembering this once-pristine island and its simple culture.

A friendly doorman advised me after I questioned him to

eat at the "Three Queens," a local favorite. It turned out to be a good choice. The service was slow (the first sign of civilization) by lovely older black women.

I had my first conch fritters (a local staple made from a large shellfish) and grouper, a succulent, flakey, white-fleshed fish. The next morning I walked the waterfront and all the old ladies selling crafts were wearing wool caps. I was so amazed I forgot to photograph them. To me it was a warm sunny day.

Back at the hotel I met Laurie, the fourth party in our group, a sweet and friendly middle-aged librarian from New Mexico, and off we all went to the airport for our trip to Cuba.

We arrived with several hours to spare. There was already a line of people with huge amounts of luggage, some looking like body bags. It was hard to believe it all could be safely stowed aboard; Cuban airlines are very lax. Later I found smoking was permitted and you could land in a reclining position.

While waiting in line to be checked in I struck up a conversation with a fellow named Harry, from Bermuda, who had a company called Enterprise submarine, Ltd. for underwater reef viewing. We exchanged business cards and I said I might be a potential investor.

The flight was scheduled to leave at 4 p.m. and it took one hour. Harry boastingly said, "If it leaves on time I'll buy you a bottle of rum." We left on time. I told him I would meet him at his hotel, the Nacional, for a drink, but I never made it.

The Havana airport was relatively quiet, but we were all exhilarated by being on Cuban soil. While standing in line for immigration, an official came out and called my name. When I acknowledged who I was, he asked in a very friendly manner in English if I were a journalist. He asked what I wrote and I told him and he smiled and went away.

We were met at the airport with a bus and drove through the suburbs to our hotel on the Malecón, Havana's curving sea wall highway and walk, where at any time of day you will see lovers facing the sea, clutched in a fervent embrace.

The island parks were very clean and the houses appeared to be well maintained in the affluent suburbs. From the beginning there was a profusion of bicycles due to the cost of gasoline and low wages.

On the bus I met Christopher, a travel writer, and his stunning black nineteen-year-old Cuban girlfriend, Daisy, which developed into a pleasant friendship.

We were taken to the Riviera Hotel. It was built by the notorious Jewish mafia tycoon Meyer Lansky in the late '50s and the Cubans were doing their best to give it a facelift. I expected to see Lucille Ball and Desi Arnaz in the lobby. Nothing was changed from the fifties, which made it glitzy and fun.

I had a spacious room overlooking the ocean. There were deep gouges in the carpet and one lampshade fell off, but the rest was in working order. (What do you expect for only $300 a night? Just kidding.)

At dinner I met the rest of our group, all friendly and mostly from California. The food was served buffet style, a variety of dishes plain but good. People commented because I used salt and had seconds. They were mostly vegetarians, a common fraternity today. I ordered espresso and settled into my first Cuban cigar. I was in Havana heaven.

Several of us went to a folkloric Afro/Cuban dance at a local school. They were good but somehow it did not seem exotic because of the setting. Two young people not connected to the group leapt into the aisle and began dancing, then onto the stage. It was very disruptive but exciting.

In the morning I grabbed a cab on my own and went off. I was not prepared for the deterioration of old Havana. It looked at times like a bombed-out city in Europe, everything seemed to be crumbling and in need of repair. Whole blocks of faded pastel buildings were gutted along the Malecón. Narrow cobblestone streets divided balconied apartment buildings. At times water would cascade into the street from above when someone was cleaning. Through all the poorness was a definite ancient charm, but you knew the tenants wished for something better.

The street was full of life and spirit and the people had great dignity. children asked for dollars, coins or Chicklets. Older people asked for money but didn't beg. Women would throw kisses at me; some would pinch me and laugh. The stores were empty and what merchandise there was looked as though it belonged in a Salvation Army Thrift Store. Pharmacies had nothing in their windows. Their counters and showcases were bare, as if the city were under siege.

I walked past the Ambus Mundo Hotel, where I had stayed and where Hemingway wrote "For Whom the Bells Toll." It was boarded up.

La Bodeguita Del Medio, a famous bar and restaurant for artists, which I had frequented when I first visited, was still going strong. It was filled with tourists and was considered very expensive by the common Cuban.

I went into the Museum of the Revolution. Admission was three dollars and three dollars to photograph. Everything was in Spanish. The photographs of the times were very interesting and there were life-sized figures of Fidel and Ché fighting in the mountains. Also caricatures of Reagan and Bush calling them "cretins."

A man stopped me on the street holding his stomach in pain and he looked terrible, so I gave him a dollar.

As I came out of the Montecristo cigar factory, which was not functioning because of remodeling, two young men approached me and one asked if I wanted to buy cigars. I said "No." Alain was the spokesperson. He knew more English and was less shy than his friend, China. both were handsome young men. They were close to the age when I first came to Cuba. Alain was twenty-five and China, twenty-seven.

Alain was around five foot, with short black hair, chiseled features and a strong physique from playing handball. China had black, curly, shoulder-length hair, hazel slanted eyes, and an infectious smile. He had a small dab of hair under his lower lip, along with a mustache that gave him a rougueish look. I knew my daughter, Josephine, would have found either attractive.

Alain brought up the subject of cigars again, now that he had gained my confidence. He said he could get me a box of 25 Montecristo No. 1 for twenty collars on the black market. In

Canada or elsewhere an individual cigar would cost twelve dollars.

After I agreed we jumped into a taxi and rattled off into a distant neighborhood. Several young men were playing handball against a building on a narrow street. Alain sprang out of the taxi and joined his friends swatting the ball on the rebound, not missing a beat.

After several frantic maneuvers the game stopped and they had a conference. One of his friends grabbed his bike leaning against a lamp post, and dashed off. Ten minutes later he returned waving a box of Montecristo No. 1s, which he handed to Alain. It was like West Side Story in Old Havana.

Alain and China tagged along, making spotty conversation, until I felt comfortable and safe with them. Alain said he was an electrician with a diploma and made 150 pesos a month, the equivalent, he said, of three dollars American. He went on to say their food was rationed and they were often without enough to eat.

We went to a plaza and I bought them a beer and listened to some musicians singing romantic ballads. Alain asked if I wanted to go to a house and hear African drummers and I said OK.

There wasn't a street, it seemed, without a policeman or two and I noticed Alain and China seemed edgy. When we arrived at the house nothing was happening. A wierd-looking young man in a tee shirt asked Alain and China for identification, obviously an undercover policeman. Alain's papers were not in order so they took him off. I left with China, gave him my card and room number at the hotel, and caught a cab.

The next day Alain called and we met. He said he had to stand for three hours with his face against a wall and his hands behind his head and was threatened to be punched. They did not feed him and he had to sleep outside on a concrete floor in his tee shirt. he was fined and released the next morning. He said it happens all the time.

Tonight would be the first night of the jazz festival at the Casa de Cultura Plaza to see Chucho Valdez e Irakere, a promi-

nent pianist, keyboardist, composer with his great salsa band
and a number of other groups that were sizzling. There were
several thousand people, all very orderly, drinking rum, happy
and proud of their culture and appreciative of the musicians.
Nearly everyone danced and sang in unison with the stage singers.

After the concert there was more music at the hotel, and
we were given tickets for at a nightclub called the "Palacio de la
Salsa." The music was non-stop. The lobby was filled with young
beautiful women, all asking to be taken into the nightclub, because it cost ten U.S. dollars, way beyond their means. Men
kept drifting in and pairing off. The hotel allowed them to have
bottles of rum in the lobby, so many small groups clustered
around buckets of ice and cans of Coca-Cola.

We were briefed by Jill, one of the organizers of our group,
that we would be approached by many young women and they
were truly not prostitutes, but destitutes because of the horren-
dous economy.

Sunday (Domingo) was another night of jazz at the Casa
de Cultura Plaza. Even with a program it was hard to follow,
because of all the Spanish names involved. The enthusiasm never
waned, the musicians were brilliant, and the audience was insa-
tiable.

The next day I took Alain and China to the beach called
Santa Maria. It was a $20 fare one way and it took at least a half
hour. The water was a Caribbean blue, but the beach was trashed.
I had to change behind some makeshift boards. An ingenuous
fellow approached us with a newspaper rolled into a cone shape.
At the end was a safety pin that he attached to a long-playing
record, which he revolved on a turntable of sorts with his finger.
Lo and behold, the young Thomas Edison produced music. If
you get very close you could understand the words of the singer,
although it was in Spanish. I felt he deserved a dollar. We nego-
tiated a $15 return fare for our taxi.

Lunes (Monday) — more jazz at the Cultural Plaza. My
favorite was Grupo Bamboleo, a close-knit jazz group that
blasted with impeccable precision. They produced incendiary

jazz. Each musician was a superb soloist. A beautiful black woman with curls cascading to her shoulders sang and danced. Two extraordinarily beautiful young dancers leapt onto the stage in the barest of costumes and gyrated as if their bodies were liquid. The crowd went wild.

A large woman next to me spoke English and Spanish fluently. I introduced myself. Her name was Iraida, a Puerto Rican from New York. She was with several Cuban men who shared their rum and ebullience with me. We danced and cheered together and had a great time. Iraida had a wonderful sense of fun.

The next day I roamed the streets of old Havana. The Central Plaza, which was so hectic in the early days, was devoid of life, no tourists. In the parks were small flea markets with barely anything for sale, mostly fittings for gas stoves and cheap plastic household utensils.

The Plaza Hotel, a venerable establishment, was still in existence, so I decided to have lunch. It still had great elegance. The dining room had a few patrons. The waitresses wore long dresses and Nikes. My waitress appeared to be my daughter's age, seventeen. She was very sweet and attentive.

That night Alain and China invited me to the Amphiteatro, a gargantuan cement tiered complex that served as a disco. It was for the masses, no tourists in sight. They paid one peso and I paid a dollar. Everyone brought their own bottles of rum, and it was 98 percent black. The band never showed up, so they just played records. Everyone danced. There were small unescorted children. A young woman in a tight-fitting sparkling blue outfit that kept creeping up on her as her body quivered and pulsated flung her hands into the air in sheer abandon and shook as though possessed. The smallest children writhed in perfect rhythm, unashamed and delighting in their bodies and the music.

After the dance Alain insisted on getting me a taxi at a bargain rate. He said I should not be on the streets alone, warning me it was very dangerous at night.

We stopped by Alain's apartment so he could get more rum and the police grabbed him. His mother was in the apartment and I did the best I could to explain the situation. Just the men-tion of police brought a customary worried look. China appeared laughing and soon Alain appeared, saying there was no "problema," his papers were in order.

On parting he said he wanted to have me for lunch the next day and he would try to catch some fish. We arranged to meet at a nearby hotel and while I was killing time, by chance I saw China on a public telephone that used operators for local calls. He was unable to reach his girlfriend, but he was charged 10 pesos.

When we arrived at Alain's apartment the meal was all prepared. The building was falling apart, but there were beautiful old Spanish tiles everywhere. Alain mentioned because it was Valentine's Day they got extra gas to cook with. It was too rough for Alain to fish, so the main dish was pork, which I love cooked Cuban style.

He showed me his fishing raft, a horseshoe-shaped inflatable about five feet long with a net flooring. He propelled himself with flippers. I couldn't imagine going out into a shark infested, treacherous sea in such a vulnerable craft.

Our meal consisted of freshly squeezed orange juice, a salad of fresh cabbage, tomatoes and green peppers, fried plantain chips, pork cooked in its own juice with lots of fresh garlic, black beans with white rice, and sweet bananas. It reminded me of my old Key West days. I almost felt guilty. I was deeply touched by Alain's generosity — it must have cost him his month's wages and rationing.

He introduced me to a petite dyed blonde girl friend across the hall called Marisal and further down the hall to a drummer named André who had long silver hair. He had thick arms from years of drumming. He complained he was old at 58, but looked quite fit. He said he taught many of the black drummers Afro/Cuban jazz, but he couldn't get work because he was white.

Alain needed rum for late night partying, so he went off with a large brown bottle and returned with it filled by someone in his building for three dollars, which I treated him to. I'm sure it only cost him a few pesos.

Walking to get a taxi, we passed through a beautiful square

surrounded by a cathedral and other old ornate buildings. Alain pointed out the street was made of wood and sure enough, on close inspection one saw that they were small blocks of wood wedged in alongside of one another. You could see the grain and some had split. They were so old and worn they had a high leathery polish to them, which made them look like cobblestones.

The square was crowded. We went into one building that had a high open center court with balconies all around. There were several cigar makers, who deftly cut long leaves of cured tobacco with a crescent-shaped flat steel blade, rolled them, and set them in molds. Often the cigar maker was puffing on one of his own creations. There was also a woman cigar maker, who was by gender much more delicate and sensual, until the knife came into play.

Returning to my hotel, I always felt somewhat guilty at dinner, having such a wide variety of food to choose from and being able to eat as much as I liked. It just wasn't fair, the haves and have-nots. I am not a missionary, but neither am I a mercenary.

The next day I had arranged with my friends Christopher and Daisy to share a car and driver and go see Hemingway's home. While waiting for them in the lobby an attractive Cuban woman I presumed to be in her mid-forties approached me and asked if I were the American writer and I said yes, nearly blushing.

Her name was Silvia González Guerra. She presented her card and underneath her name it said *autor musical*. Among other talents she was a composer. We had a lengthy and interesting conversation and she gave me a cassette titled *Bienvido a Cuba Bella*. Two of the nine recorded songs were hers. She recommended a driver with a car and we set out for Poppa Hemingway's home. We played Silvia's tape along the way; it was very romantic.

On the outskirts of Havana we stopped at the main city market. It was a block square building with a series of stalls to accommodate the vendors. The first thing I noticed was someone crushing sugar cane and selling the juice by the glass, which

I had throughout the Caribbean and have always enjoyed. It was very refreshing, with an earthy aftertaste.

This was a recent reversal in policy, to allow the farmers to sell their produce on the free market. It was the most produce I had seen, although even here there was not an abundance. On a main street in the city vendors had little to offer and the vegetables looked poorly.

Everyone was very friendly as I waved and photographed. The whole carcass of a calf, stripped of its hide, lay on a table, a deep purple, head intact, with veins, muscles and sinews. It looked very sacrificial. A group of men posed for me with a turkey on a rope, which they offered to me for fifteen dollars, while a pig grunted next to us. Garlands of sausages looked like fat rosaries. There was no pace or excitement, and there were few shoppers, men sat in groups, talking.

We went on to Hemingway's house. It reminded me of when I saw Hemingway drinking at the La Floridita restaurant in Havana and my brother Willy having met Hemingway at a bar in Key West.

The admission to the property was $5 and although you could not go into the house, each photograph of the interior from a doorway or window cost $5; very strange indeed. It was a rather modest sprawling home perched on a hill looking off toward Havana. There were ample grounds. It must have been very secluded and private when Ernest lived there. Now the surrounding area was crowded.

The interior looked very comfortable. The walls were lined with books and every room had trophy heads of animals he had shot in Africa. His wife, Mary, had built him his own ivory tower, a separate tower building close to the house where he could be alone to write, but it was said he never liked it or used it much.

In the back part of the property was an empty swimming pool, the graves and headstones of three of his pet dogs, and his boat, the Pilar, under cover. It was a handsome wooden launch and it was easy to visualize the many happy days of fishing it provided him.

Our congenial driver, Miguel, suggested we go to a nearby

restaurant called La Terrazza in Cohimar, which Hemingway frequented and formed his story for "The Old Man and the Sea."

The town itself, situated on a bay, did not look very promising. When we entered the restaurant I felt I was transported back in time. It reminded me of the beautiful old cafes of Havana, with handmade furniture and high ceilings with revolving fans. A long bar polished to perfection held a good assortment of liquors. The floor was terrazzo, and large glass windows allowed in sunlight and sea air. On the walls were numerous photographs of Hemingway presenting a trophy to Fidel Castro for winning a bill fish tournament sponsored by Hemingway.

We were served complimentary drinks made with blue Curacao in honor of the Old Man and the Sea. The only customers in the place were Cubans at a large table, which made it all seem very real.

After lunch I photographed a bronze bust of Hemingway near the bar. I asked Daisy to put her black hand with an assortment of silver rings at the base and it turned out to be a very striking photograph.

We were all full from our lunches and decided to walk around the town. I wanted to be alone and suspected Christopher and Daisy felt the same.

Some of the older, more interesting buildings were falling apart from neglect. A group of women asked me to photograph them, which I did, knowing they would never see the picture. It turned out to be one of my better photographs, full of joy and life.

In a vacant lot behind a fence a group of men were playing dominoes. I stopped and watched and within minutes they tried to communicate. I had the best time with my few words of Spanish and was encouraged to photograph. When I left it was like leaving old friends.

A small group of children approached me, laughing, shouting and enjoying themselves. They didn't ask for anything, but I gave them all of my change. There was a smattering of English as they walked along with me and gathered new friends along the way. They were curious and affectionate and I photographed them on a sea wall near a small fort. In that short time I felt very attached and thought about my own grown children.

The next day we went to the National School of Art, where they hold the music and dance workshops. Chucho Valdez gave a talk, then played a thrilling composition on the piano. The school has survived because of devoted people like Chucho and the Music and Dance Program. Many professors have graduated from the school, so they in turn teach to show their appreciation. The blockade is getting worse and the subsidies are being withdrawn, so more outside help is needed.

Caribbean Music and Dance has brought many students. There are currently 600 students enrolled in the music course and 150 in the dance course. It is the only school of modern dance. The acceptance of students is based on their ability; there is no charge for the courses. The Caribbean Music and Dance Program has donated instruments and medicine.

The National School of the Arts was established in 1960. There is also a course on Circus Arts. It is amazing how young and talented the assortment of students are. The open-air hallways were flooded with practicing students, even a tuba player. We watched drummers, saxophone players, singers and dancers perform in their classrooms.

One of the more interesting classes was being given by Richard Egües, master flutist and composer, one of the original members of the famous band Orquesta Aragón and known for his facility with dance forms such as the danzón, chucha and charanga.

I left the school with a sense of hope, prompted by these gifted people, and I realized how important the cultural exchange is and that it must not be involved with politics.

A strong heart is not achieved by exercise alone; it is by giving and receiving. I only want to hear the music.

Leaving Cuba was sad, leaving my friends behind trapped in uncertainty, only their hope, dignity and humor sustains them. The Cuban people are stars in their own small stellar system, kept in place by the gravitational pull of poverty and oppression. Fidel Castro has given them a sense of worth, good education and medical care, and a sense of their own self-esteem. What they need now is economic help, freedom of expression, and the lifting of our embargo so they can help themselves and be free to travel and still retain the pride of their incredible culture.

On my return to Nassau with my friends Laurie and John, we were all euphoric with our individual experiences. Nassau seemed drab after Cuba and I was able to make a connecting flight.

When I went through U.S. customs I worried about my Montecristo and Romeo y Julieta cigars being confiscated. It was rumored that they were fakes, but my Montecristo was sweet and delicate and it held a long ash, proof of its goodness. I was ready to put up a stiff fight if they threatened to take them away. I had a document saying as a journalist I was able to bring $500 in purchases, plus cigars, back to the States.

The U.S. Customs inspectors asked how long I had stayed and I said "a week in Cuba." I had said the wrong thing — he didn'tt know I had been to Cuba. I had not looked at my passport. As a courtesy Cuba had not stamped it. He asked what I had brought back and I told him. He asked to see the contents of my luggage after I told him about the cigars.

He asked what kinds of books I had written and I told him. He showed a genuine interest, gave me a wink, and said, "OK." I thanked him and felt very proud to be American and part of the Americas and went dashing off to my next flight.

Cuba Revisited '95

My last visit to Cuba was in February and the experience was so intense and rewarding that I began to plan another trip as soon as I returned.

Nassau was my destination. My tickets on Air Cubana through Baha Tours were waiting there for me.

A dear friend, Silvia Gonzalez Guerra, who I had met on my previous trip, had agreed to be my guide and translator. She was to meet me at the airport.

Although my flight was an hour late, my ever-faithful friend Silvia was waiting at the airport. Her dark eyes flashed and she had a wide, warm smile. As we embraced, Silvia gushed a mixture of Spanish and English.

I was introduced to Oscar, our chauffeur. A middle-aged man, he kept an indefatigable sense of humor throughout my two-week stay.

The humid, tropical night air engulfed me in a steamy embrace.

As we drove into the heart of the city, we encountered various stages of blackouts. Our headlights illuminated droves of people on bicycles. More often than not, a companion rode on the crossbar or a rear seat. Because gasoline is over $4 dollars a gallon, and the incomes so low, every street corner was filled with people waiting for buses.

Professional people earn four hundred pesos a month. With

an exchange rate of 20 pesos to the dollar and most everything purchased in dollars, great hardships were everywhere.

Silvia suggested I stay with a variety of people in their homes. They needed the income and I could meet more people and broaden my cultural experience. The arrangement appealed to me.

Our first stop was at Adelaida's, a friend of Silvia and a well-known and respected Cuban artist.

We walked four flights up to an open garden apartment filled with plants and the artistry of Adelaida. She was a beautiful mulatto and I was immediately bewitched.

Cockateels, parrots and a canary occupied various cages.

Later Adelaida's nephew, Manola, coaxed a turtle from under the furniture.

When Silvia's 'esposo' Oscar Pla, arrived we became friends instantly. He was also an artist and later in the evening presented me with a miniature construction of a Havana street scene. Adelaida made fresh limeade to which I added generous portions of rum.

The conversation was lively with Silvia doing a great job of interpreting.

Adelaida had created the apartment out of found objects and her inexhaustible creativity. There seemed to be no medium in which she did not express her art. She showed me drawings, large paintings, ceramics, terra cotta, fabric design, leather work and amazing silver jewelry.

Adelaida had lived all over Europe, notably Spain, but found it to be racist.

A late dinner of chicken, rice and perfectly spiced black beans, followed by fresh papaya and Cuban coffee laced with rum, put me in a state of bliss.

After a soothing shower (the shower walls were imbedded with green bottles), I fell into a large bed, happy and relaxed. A fan oscillated, tenderly playing a cool breeze over my naked body.

Silvia came by in the morning as I was sipping fresh papaya juice. We made a tour of hotels, the Hemingway marina and boutiques.

Only in the past year has Castro allowed the people to open small businesses. They have rented rooms, served meals in their homes and sold confections on the streets in front of their homes.

Some women were selling coffee and I ordered some. Since I didn't have pesos, they graciously offered it to me.

At one store front, people were pushing and shoving to buy slices of a heavily frosted cake.

Because the South American Explorers Club in Ithaca, NY, had promised to publish the story I had written from my previous trip, an possibly a sequel, I kept copious notes as I wandered the streets.

While on my own I tried a restaurant that was very busy and the menu was in dollars. I ordered some risotto and another dish—layers of cheese oozing with oil and stuffed with raw meat. Neither was edible!

Two people next to me ordered a table full of assorted items and I wondered how they could afford it.

I tried the Habana Libre Hotel and ate in a restaurant that Adelaida had designed. It was very beautiful with a tropical atmosphere, but the food was terrible.

Silvia gave me the name of the writers' union of Cuba. It was in a very old and beautiful building. A conference was in progress, but I was invited to read from my books when I returned to Cuba.

A man stopped me on the street and asked me, in English, to take a letter back to the States for him. I gave him my address from a slip of paper I was carrying, but he never showed up.

On almost every block, someone offered to sell me rum or cigars. Once, in an effort to put the salesman off, I pretended to speak Russian. He did not appear gullible and kept laughing at me.

Silvia kept me busy with endless excursions to monuments and museums and also introduced me to many artists and musicians.

When I had visited in February, I attended a performance by a group called "Bamboleo." At the top of my list for this trip was to hear and see them again and to meet the members of the group.

Miraculously, it happened!

After meeting Lazaro Valdez, the leader, I invited him to lunch at Adelaida's. He brought his father, also named Lazaro, and a drummer called Luis.

Lazaros' father is the musical director at the Nacional Hotel. He was very fit, witty and outgoing.

Thanks to Silvia's amazingly quick translations, the conversation flowed smoothly and Adelaida's food was superb.

Lazaro invited me to two of his performances and asked me to write the liner for his new CD.

Silvia, Oscar, and a new acquaintance, a young ballerina accompanied me to the first performance. My name was announced to a wild crowd of enthusiastic fans. Lazaro provided rum and we danced ourselves into a frenzy. My companion, who called herself "Chocolate," was the best dancer I have ever experienced.

The Salsa music was torrid. There was a combination of 13 performers including three singers. Two female mulattos were not only sensational looking with shaved heads and unbelievable figures, but were excellent singers and dancers. A very competent male counterpart completed the trio.

The arrangements were flawless. On his keyboard, Lazaro coolly presided over what seemed chaotic tempos, transforming them into a pulsating tangle of mad rhythms. The rest of the group floated and swayed as the crowd yelled, screamed and crowded the dance floor.

Returning a week later for another performance, I was accompanied by another dancer, more subdued because she had the flu. We joined Sven, a German friend I had met at the first performance. He was a free lance journalist and photographer doing articles for DerSpeigaland Stern.

This performance was as raucaus as the first and we had to shout to make ourselves heard. However, it was not nearly as deafening as the discos!

I presented one of my signed books to Lazaro and this

prompted a very emotional farewell with much hugging and rapid translations of good-bye.

Also performing at the first concert of Bambaleo was an all-girls band called Anacaona. They were dazzling—all beautiful and clad in sequined, skin-tight mini dresses. In addition, each was a top musician and performer. They invited me to two rehearsals before they left on a tour of Jamaica.

On my last visit, I had also met Chucho Valdes, a famous jazz pianist, keyboardist, arranger and composer, who had a swinging orchestra that toured Europe, Canada and South America.

We went to visit Chucho and found him hanging out in the street with friends. This gave me an opportunity to get some good photos of him and Silvia photographed the two of us together.

At that night's concert, I presented him with one of my books and a T-shirt.

The crowd was wild—people dancing in their seats and then in the aisles. Small children flooded the aisles gyrating—it was obvious that they had danced out of the womb!

Each day with Silvia was a pleasure and an adventure. She was loved by everyone.

We went to see her son Cristo Benito, a tenor, rehearse for "Carmen." His troupe was to give a performance in Havana in a few weeks and then go to Europe.

The dance sequence for the ballerinas was about to begin and the young and fit dancers were stretching in their skin-tight leotards, chattering with one another and some embracing. Flustered but firm, the dancemaster shouted and slammed a stick on the stage to get their attention. A record was placed on the phonograph and a very tinny and scratchy sound was produced. The beautiful young bodies fell into cadence.

This is when I first saw Chocolate, a petite black woman with a perfect dancer's figure.

Cristo never sang but we did hear the leading man, a baritone, sing an aria with the soprano Carmen.

As the rehearsal ended, I asked some of the ballerinas if I

could photograph them. They were all friendly and obliging, especially Chocolate. Silvia invited her to come along with us.

That night I took her to a cabaret at the Habana Libre Hotel with my new friends Manolo and Marlene, who were now acting as my hosts.

Earlier I had gone with Manola to the Habana-Riviera Hotel where I had stayed on my last trip. I purchased a bottle of light run for Mojitos, a national drink made with rum, sugar, fresh lime juice and herbal buena (good grass), a form of fresh mint leaves. The ingredients are crushed and topped off with carbonated water and sometimes a dash of Angostura bitters.

I offered drinks to Manolo's extended family so we finished off the bottle and left in a dancing mood.

The floor show was typical with a group of male comedians doing pantomimes and an orchestra with scantily clad dancers and singers, One of the comedians dressed as a woman, came out into the audience and pretended to kiss me, causing an uproar.

While Chocolate and Marlene were in the ladies room, the female dancers came into the audiences to pick out partners for a dance contest. One chose me!

My partner was a tall beautiful brunette. The rum had relaxed me and I did some elaborate steps with my lovely companion as the band played.

Each of the five couples in the contest had our turn and then the audience judged which was the best. We won!

The ladies returned and we excused ourselves to go to the men's room. Rather than return to the table when we were finished, Manalo took me across the street to a discotheque that was in full swing.

I started dancing with a beautiful young girl and her friend. We had to leave and she kissed me good-bye.

When we returned to Chocolate and Marlene, they asked why we were gone so long. We just laughed and poured them some rum.

A friend of Chocolate's came and asked her to dance. The only couple on the floor, they were sensational under the spotlight. Chocolate was better than anyone in the show and the audience went crazy for her.

After leaving the club, I bought a copy of the *International Herald Tribune*—the first news I had since leaving the States.

On the last page was an article by Mike Zwerin, a musician and writer friend I had not seen in over 20 years. We had dated the same girl, Vicki, a tenant in my building. She was working for Bert Stern, who took the last photographs of Marilyn Monroe.

When I returned home I wrote to Mike at his Paris office to catch up on the intervening years.

The next day, Silvia took me to meet Angel Diaz, the originator of a bolero-style musical movement of the '40s called "Feeling." He was a very youthful and energetic man in his early 60s. He played his guitar and sang for us. It was very touching.

I bought one of his tapes, "Es Feeling Y Es Bolero," on which he sang with a large orchestra. It was very romantic band I could understand his earlier popularity.

Like most Cuban artists, time has past them by and they live sparsely—but they have amazing spirit.

We then went to visit Lili, the first woman glass blower in Cuba. She was a handsome woman with a warm personality.

She had only a few glass pieces to show us, but she also had oil painting and ceramics.

I was honored and touched by her generosity when she presented me a gift of two small ceramic folklore figurines of a man and woman dancing.

When I began to feel the need to get back in touch with nature and the countryside, Silvia suggested driving out to Las Terrazas tourist complex. A reserve of the Biosphere in the Sierra del Rosairo mountains, it is located at the northeastern tip of the Pinar del Rio province only an hour west of Havana.

The lush countryside revived me and repaired the wear of many late nights in Havana!

Farmers with horsedrawn carts were on the highway. A rugged looking campesino walked along the road carrying a machete and a bundle of rope looped around his shoulder.

When Oscar stopped the car and asked the man if I could photograph him, he was very friendly and gave me a wide grin.

We climbed up the mountains and turned in at a guard gate. The guard lifted the large metal arm and let us pass.

Part of the preserve had been a coffee plantation during the 19th century.

We stopped for lunch at the main house, which had been turned into a restaurant. Other guests were three German tourists and their guide.

The buildings were made of local salmon-colored stones and had intricate tile roofs.

We drove on to the Moka Hotel, a four-star establishment which blends into the landscape.

I knew that I wanted to stay.

My large room had a marble bath, satellite TV, and elegant contemporary furnishings. The cost was $58, also in force during the high season.

At the reserve are cabanas on small lakes and 850 inhabitants who are part of a rural community founded in 1971 by the government. The purpose is regional development including forest preservation and rescue of the area's natural and cultural values.

Silvia and Oscar left me in good hands. The manager, Jose R. Porrata Maury, assured me that I would be comfortable and that he would arrange for me to do some fishing.

A young man named Hoti was assigned as my guide. Since he spoke fluent English, he was able to answer my many questions.

I decided on a swim in the pool which was a short walk from the main lodge. No one was in sight and I learned later that I was the only guest.

The staff was friendly and helpful. The chef gave me an herbal concoction as a welcome drink.

Hoti took me around to meet the craftsmen and artists, all of whom seemed genuinely happy and pleased with their life styles. Within the compound were a wood carver, Hoti's brother Lester, a gifted painter, and women and children weaving animals, handbags and hats from reeds.

At night, we went to the musical director's house where he played guitar while others played bongos and clavas. As they sang, dogs and small children ran in and out of the room. I danced with the director's sister, a wonderful woman, full of life.

After the little concert, we all went to the disco and drank rum. Some of the women asked me to dance.

A fishing trip to a small dammed lake nestled among the hills, had been arranged for the next day. The manager said I would catch "trucha," trout.

Alberto, my guide, took me into a shop to pick out some lures. Mepps, Rappelas, spinners, floating and diving plugs that rattled—they were all American, so I was familiar with them.

We pushed off in a small rowboat. The rod was too large but I managed to get it under control and shortly landed a nearly three-pound fish they called "trucha." It was in fact, a large mouth bass called "El robalo!"

In just a couple of hours of fishing, I landed two other smaller ones and hooked a Tilapia, which fell off just as I hauled him over the side.

While I was fishing, the heat built up and the humidity pressed down on us. I removed a light jacket and reached into my camera bag for a long-billed fishing cap. As I pulled it out, a roll of exposed film which was caught in it, fell in the water. Alberto and I watched helplessly as it disappeared into the pale brown water, shimmering in its descent. I wandered what priceless scenes and friends I was losing.

When I mentioned it to the manager, he sympathized and gave me a fresh roll of slide film.

He was impressed with my catch and invited me into his office for good strong coffee. He asked me to represent the resort in the states. I said I would be happy to, but given the embargo and current situation between our governments, I couldn't figure out how to attract American tourists.

Hoti had arranged lunch at a local woman's apartment.

She prepared a traditional Cuban feast with pork as the main course. Her son served us and Hoti acted as interpreter. In the short time we sat drinking coffee, we became friends and I kissed her good-bye as we left.

I was all for Hoti's suggestion that we rent motor scooters and go up into the mountains. My scooter was a constant source of trouble and kept stalling.

We turned off the highway onto dirt roads playing a sort of tag, constantly overtaking each other, and laughing all the way.

We arrived at a place where two men were making charcoal. A thin, shrivelled man was putting the fuel into burlap sacks. Two goats were tethered near him. Cut logs were strewn everywhere in the clearing with thick tropical vegetation on all sides and mountains in the background.

A second man prepared a charcoal mound in a symmetrical design. The fire was dropped in a hole at the center of the mound and the whole artistic creation smoldered for days to form the charcoal.

The scene brought to mind a favorite photographer of mine—Sebastiao Salgado. The Brazilian-born artist depicted the cruel working conditions of indigenous people around the world.

The difference was that these people were happy, healthy and did not have a cruel overseer. They worked at their own prescribed pace.

We continued back up into the hills to see the ruins of a coffee plantation. It had been raining heavily so the streams flooded the roads. Hoti skidded and fell of his scooter. As I looked back after him, I went off the road and stopped abruptly in the brambles at the edge of a deep chasm.

We came to a swollen stream and left the scooters to wade through a strong current to the ruins in the jungle.

On the way home, we stopped at a mountain stream. I plunged in and swam and sat under a water fall, getting a free, natural massage.

The next morning at breakfast, my waiter asked me to mail a letter to his girlfriend. A middle-aged Cuban couple were the only other diners. It was 8 a.m. and they were smoking and ordered beer!

I remembered it was Hoti's birthday, so when he arrived I

gave him a tip.

As we were leaving, the Cuban couple pointed out that I had dropped some money—it turned out to be a $5 bill!

The hotel did not accept American credit cards, so I had to cash travelers checks to pay my lodging bill.

At my request, Hoti took me to say good-bye to a lovely young lady who worked at the hotel. We had danced the previous night at the disco.

Hoti arranged for a Toyota Land Cruiser to take me back to Havana and he insisted on coming along.

When Silvia met me at the Nacional Hotel we kissed and embraced as though we had been parted for a long time.

She took me to the home of her friend Omar Gonzalez, who worked in leather. Before leaving, I placed an order for some sandals.

Recently divorced, Omar was now happily involved with an attractive woman. He showed us pictures of her and told of his plans to turn his apartment into a restaurant and bar.

Silvia and Omar kissed and embraced both in greeting and on leaving.

We then went to visit Omar and Martha Gonzolez, both of whom work for Manos, an art magazine about Cuban artists.

He said he was going to publish a magazine in December about popular Cuban music and musicians. When he asked if I would be interested in representing them in the states, I replied with an enthusiastic, "YES!"

Often in discussions with artists, the current hardships were mentioned, but they never whined or seemed to be afraid to talk about their plight. Always, they were optimistic about the future.

After having some good coffee, Omar and I promised to correspond and Silvia and I left.

At a small, family-run restaurant, we ate in the family's diningroom as children watched television in an overstuffed chair.

Several members of the family prepared the food in a tiny, crowded kitchen. Everyone was friendly and in a good mood.

The husband, another "Lazaro," catered to our every need.

When we had entered, a beautiful young woman had given me a wonderful open smile. When I mentioned her to Silvia, she asked me if I would like to meet her and of course I agreed! Her name was Yordanka and she spoke some English.

After an introduction and getting acquainted, I invited her to dinner the following evening. We were to meet at the restaurant which was only a few houses from where I was staying.

At 9 p.m., I left my apartment to find Yordanka standing outside with an older woman who looked like Lena Horne in her prime. She introduced her mother, Sonia.

Not knowing what else to do, I invited her to dinner, thinking she might leave after assuring herself that her daughter was in good, safe company.

Her mother was beautiful and charming and I was flattered to have such attractive companions.

When the subject of dancing came up it was obvious that her mother wanted to come along. I invited her but told them I was not sure if I had enough money.

We took a taxi that cost $7 to the Comodoro Hotel. The entrance was crowded with beautiful young women hoping to find a benefactor to pay the $10 entrance fee and take them in.

To get a table near the dance floor it was necessary to buy a bottle of rum for $40. We sat in the bar and ordered drinks because I did not have enough cash.

In no time, it became crowded and I took turns dancing with Yordanka and Sonia. The music was so loud it was impossible to carry on a conversation. The decor was very modern with psychedelic lights pulsating.

It was nearly 3 a.m. when we gave up.

I was considering going to Varadero Beach and Yordanka wanted to go with me (without her mother). My plans changed however, and when I called her she was disappointed. She gave me her address and phone number and invited me to stay with her when I returned to Havana.

I still hadn't purchased cigars so Silvia took me to a friend's house in old Havana.

We were greeted by a middle-aged woman who offered coffee and gave me a cigar from a factory where she had previously worked.

After a long wait, her daughter, who had worked with Silvia at the Habana Libre Hotel, arrived. She was unbelievably beautiful with thick auburn hair. Silvia joked with her, telling her she should get a divorce and marry me.

She was kind enough to give me a flattering and affectionate smile that satisfied me and stayed in my memory for days.

Her handsome young husband soon arrived with many boxes of assorted black market cigars.

I selected several boxes of Cohibas (Castro's favorite) and Montecristos. In gratitude and friendship, his wife kissed me on both cheeks and I left a happy man.

The next day I moved in with a professor of hydraulics and his wife, a professor of physics at the University of Havana. Their three grown children were living in Miami, but they chose to stay behind.

In the afternoon I went to the Nacional Hotel for a massage and played a game of ping pong with the masseur. He gave me a very hard rub down and began rubbing my eyelids. Before I could tell him to stop he rubbed both of my soft contact lenses out of my eyes. Although they were not damaged, he was very apologetic and embarrassed.

On my way out, I saw two beautiful young women exercising on machines. When I stopped to watch they invited me to join them. No amount of exercising could have gotten me into the remarkable shape they were in!

Oscar's birthday was that day and I was invited to celebrate with dinner at Silvia's. Her mother, Lyma, a large woman, greeted me.

Silvia had prepared a feast. I was never able to figure out how she managed to find the time do all those wonderful and time consuming gestures.

Oscar took me next door and we drank rum with an artist friend. In the sliver of a courtyard shared by the houses, Christo serenaded me with operatic and Cuban songs.

I couldn't remember when I had been so happy and contented.

The following afternoon, we visited Rafart (Escultor Orfebre—a silver sculptor), a handsome, strong-looking, and very affable gentleman.

On one of the tables was a full-sized rooster worked in silver. Feather for feather it was impeccable in design and beauty!

His apartment was the most elegant I had seen in Cuba, with works of art everywhere. The penthouse apartment was complete with a glassed-in aviary with colorful birds fluttering and chirping inside.

I photographed him as he graciously showed us around.

There was a photograph of his younger brother who had passed away. He was also an artist.

A young man served us good coffee und Rafart invited us back for dinner when I returned to Havana.

I took an early morning walk to the University of Havana, an extremely impressive institution. Its massive stone steps lead into courtyards filled with trees, bushes and flowers and surrounded by old European style buildings. Numerous groups of students were enjoying each other's company, studying, and lounging on the old stone walls.

Located high on a hill, it offers a sweeping view of the city and the ocean in the distance.

In the afternoon, we visited Juan Capote, a wood sculptor, and his wife Theresa. Juan is a handsome and fit man in his late 50s who wears a ponytail, making him look like and Indian warrior.

All of his work was at an exhibit in Europe so I could only look at photos of his sculptures.

Juan lamented the embargo and told me of his desire to visit the United States. But for now, he knew it was a dream.

Around the corner lived Maria Antonieta, a most attractive and popular singer. She was very cordial and flirtatious. On her walls were large photographers of her taken when she appeared in a television spectacular. She blooked very much like a Hollywood star.

She invited me back the following day for a photographic session and when I arrived she looked very seductive in a white silk blouse with lace cutouts. She posed with her Pekinese dog and parrot. She was in an agreeable mood so the shoot was gratifying and fun.

I put a tissue over my flash and managed to get some lovely soft-toned photographs. It was easy to understand her popularity as I listened to the romantic cassette which she gave me.

She left the next day for a two-month tour in Venezuela.

As we traveled through the suburbs, it seemed that there were beautiful women at every street corner. Many waved and gave quick flashing smiles.

Ela Calvo, another singer, was just leaving as we arrived at her home, but she obligingly posed against a stone wall for a photo. She and Silvia are old friends so they chatted while I snapped a dozen pictures.

Ela is a large black woman, stunning dynamic and vivacious. She was glistening with body oils and her smile was radiant. Her large white teeth were offset with several gold ones.

A male entertainer friend came along, so I took more pictures.

She was late for an appointment, but said she would be singing that night at a club called Two Gardenias. We promised to go.

She had given her handbag to Silvia to hold while I photographed her. In the confusion she left without it.

Silvia and Ocar accompanied me to the night club along with Teresa, a beautiful mulatto Chinese introduced to me by Oscar the cab driver.

An out-of-work psychologist, Teresa, 33, was incredibly exotic with a good figure, high cheek bones, a bronze complexion and shiny raven-colored hair. Bubbling over with the joy of life, she wore a Chinese silk mini dress with elegant platform shoes. I knew I was a very fortunate man to enjoy her company.

The Two Gardenias was reminiscent of the late 40s and early 50s.

When we arrived a woman who looked 90 years old, was

playing exquisite boleros on the piano.

I was introduced to a wonderful comedian who appeared later and announced my name to the audience. He recited Longfellow in English and did a take off on Victor Borga.

A succession of guest singers who had been popular back in the early 50s, sang romantic ballads, backed up by prerecorded music. The audience was hushed in adulation.

When Ela Calvo sang, she was as dynamic as I had expected—earthy, intense and deeply romantic!

It was my last night in Cuba and I was feeling sad, but doing my best not to let it show.

Teresa insisted on coming with Silvia and Oscar the next morning to take me to the airport.

We stopped at Adelaida's and she presented me with three beautiful drawings done especially for me. As we embraced, it was all I could do to keep back the tears.

Because we had time to spare, we stopped near the airport at the home of Silvia's aunt and uncle. She was so loving toward them, holding her uncle's hand as she told me how kind he was to her when she was a little girl and how much she loved him.

They cut down a grapefruit and squeezed fresh juice. They also harvested huge avocados for Silvia to take home.

The effects of the humidity and the previous late night were taking their toll on me so Silvia suggested a nap. They put a fan in their own bedroom and I fell asleep almost immediately to the sound of distant Spanish-speaking voices.

I was glad my flight to Nassau was on time since I did not want a long good-bye. Teresa hugged and kissed me, whispering words of endearment in Spanish.

I began to choke up as I hugged Silvia and kissed her on both cheeks. Oscar gave me a strong bear hug and I shook hands with Oscar the chauffeur. As I was going up the escalator, Silvia call up that she loved me and would miss me. I assured her that I felt the same.

It had been a long time since I had received so much love!

As in the past, the Cubans had not stamped my passport

and when I arrived in Nassau, the immigration officials suggested they follow suit. That way the U.S. Customs would not know I had left Nassau.

Since I could not make my connection,I had to spend the night in Nassau. It was depressing after Cuba—no culture, just rich American college kids doing the limbo in one of the bars.

When I returned home, I read a NewYorkTimes article about Angela Davis, a political activist of the 60s, that said she had been in Cuba while I was there. She is presently teaching philosophy at Vassar where my son Nevin attends college.

Oddly enough, before the invasion of Grenada, I had been there vacationing with my family while she was also there as a political activist with Fidel Castro.

She is now involved in a United States/Cuba Medical Project which has just donated $5 million dollars worth of medicine to the Cuban people with no politics involved.

From my personal experience I saw that the pharmacies were out of medicine, the shelves were bare and the Cuban people were desperate for medical help.

Ms. Davis was warm and friendly when I called her, putting me in contact with the project director, Leslie Gagen.

My intentions are to get some of the local college students involved in the project.

Loving the Cuban people as I do, I am grateful to have the opportunity to help them in a humanitarian way.

CUBA (A Journal 1996)

It was my fifth trip to Cuba. I was spending my 69th birth-day there and participating in my second International Latin Jazz Festival and seeing many musician friends and other close friends. My ticket to Havana was waiting for me in Nassau with little time to spare.

Much to my dismay my suitcase was missing. After frantic efforts U.S. Air wired its Maryland office, where I made the change from Syracuse. They said it would be on the next flight.

I wanted to believe them. The person who had my Havana flight ticket said he would forward it to Havana if it didn't ar-rive on the next flight. I never saw him again after purchasing the ticket. To my amazement, I spotted my suitcase on the con-veyor belt, snatched it, and dashed for Havana Tours. Nassau customs waved me through when I excitedly explained my situ-ation.

I was the last to check in. I was carrying my camera bag and a carry-on full of presents for Cuban friends, including a typewriter for my friend Silvia. The flight only took an hour; Still I had time to unwind. At the Havana airport I had to get a visa for 30 days, which cost $15. At first the woman didn't want to give me one for that long, but I charmed her. Because of the delay, Silvia; Oscar, her spouse; and a girlfriend were waiting anxiously. My girlfriend, Yardonka, was crying, but Silvia was the first to greet me and kiss me. Next came an emotional, unwarranted outpouring from Yardonka and bear hugs from Oscar. Yardonka's mother, Sonia, hovered in the background unnoticed, and came forward and kissed me.

Silvia was the only one who spoke English, so there were hasty translations between caresses and mutual exchange. We went to a *paladar* for dinner. These are family restaurants which Castro is now allowing to operate. The more successful ones make more in a day then a doctor makes in a month.

The setting was a beautiful, old, high ceilinged turn-of-the-century home in the suburbs. We all had drinks and a delicious dinner of shrimp, pork and fish, dessert and coffee. The bill was $33 for the five of us. Silvia had arranged a beautiful five-room apartment for me that cost $25 for the night. There was a balcony overlooking the city. The warm night air, the stars and near absence of cars made it all very exotic and exciting to be back.

The next day I was invited to Yardonka's for lunch. Sonia, her attractive mother, went running, and Yardonka, her young sister, Marisa, and I went shopping. We bought cooking oil and assorted luxuries that came to over 50 U.S. dollars. Shopping was a revelation, not to be compared to a supermarket in the U.S. but well stocked. All the prices were in U.S. dollars and the store was crowded; the prices were on a par with U.S. prices, many more expensive. Since most people earn the equivalent of ten dollars a month, I could not figure out where they were getting the dollars.

Yardonka's grandparents shared the apartment and did the cooking. They had chickens on their balcony for future meals. Some neighbor showed up. I was the honored guest to be shown off.

Silvia came by and shared our meal and said we had to go to the Music Institute to register a song that we both had collaborated on. It was going to be performed by my friend Lozaro, who had a hot salsa band called *Bamboleo*. It was obvious I was expected to be on 24-hour duty by Yardonka, which did not appeal to me, so Silvia explained that "business" got top priority and I would contact Yardonka in a few days.

The next day, Feb. 9th, was my birthday, and a small party had been arranged for me at Silvia's friend Adelaida's rooftop apartment. I had stayed on a previous trip with Adelaida, a lovely attractive artist who worked in many mediums. My daughter Josephine had given me two books and an affectionate letter reminding me it was the year of the libido.

Present were a woman friend from Argentina, an architect I had met on my last visit, Lazaro of *Bamboleo* came with a musician friend, and a young ballet dancer who was to be my companion for the evening. Oscar baked a very elaborate cake and I received an assortment of very personal artistic presents, all made in my honor. It was hard to hold back tears as I blew out the candles.

I was invited to one of the Bamboleo performances. Lazaro always has several guests and buys numerous bottles of rum. His band is sensational. It wasn't long before I was on the floor gyrating, grinding and sweating, sharing Lazaro's manager's two girlfriends, one very dark and the other part Oriental, who was a challenge to my capabilities. There was an outstanding series of concerts featuring Afro Cuban Jazz. Churcho Valdes, an internationally admired Cuban jazz pianist, put together a blazing performance including a children's choir. Also featured was an American jazz trumpeter, Roy Hargrove.

Taxis can be quite cheap if you can speak Spanish, which I cannot, so Silvia or Oscar did all the negotiating with the illegal taxis. Some of the government tourist taxis with meters were not all that expensive. Bicycles are the main mode of transportation. They can also be silent killers. At night you don't hear them and none of them use lights.

During the daytime one would observe the most amusing sights. Passengers reading newspapers, babies squeezed in between nonchalant parents, passengers balanced precariously on handlebars. Some dressed in suit and tie. One woman casually plucked the lint off her jacket while her husband pedaled. Some carried long boards, boxes, and furniture, making it appear more like a circus act.

This trip there were fewer blackouts, but one did occur on

my birthday, so to me it was all the more romantic. Candles and kerosene lamps reflected on the faces of my friends as I sat in the shadows thinking about forgotten years.

My favorite *paladar* was *Los Amigos,* across from the Victorian Hotel in an alleyway. Lazaro, the robust owner, always greeted me with a strong handclasp and a hearty greeting: *Hey, Amigo!* The food was consistently good, cooked by Alicia, a large, happy black woman. I became such a regular that upon arriving I would go to the kitchen, which was open to the family dining room. With grease sputtering in the frying pan and sweat pouring from her glistening face, Alicia said something to me in Spanish as we embraced and I kissed her on both cheeks.

They treated me like a celebrity. I was always introduced around and shown off. A waitress and a waiter on different shifts spoke English and often some of the patrons spoke a little English. The dishes were mainly pork, ham, and fish, and on occasion shrimp and lobster, which were hard to come by. My cocktails were *Cuba Libres* (rum, coke and lime), sometimes three, and the bill was about seven dollars.

By comparison, drinks at the newest hotel, the *Cohiba*, a very modern hotel catering to the rich international set and a few wealthy Cubans, cost $5 each. It was like being in another country. Beautiful and expensively dressed women spoke Italian, French, German and other languages. Men puffed expansively on large Cuban cigars, conducting business over drinks.

I cruised through dining rooms where chefs in tall, pleated white hats grilled steaks and cooked assorted seafoods to order. The stations were piled high with fresh fruits and cheeses from around the world and mounds of elaborate desserts that diners piled on their plates with no room to spare.

Fountains bubbled among gay laughter while waiters poured wines of the world.

It all made me very uncomfortable after just having left *Los Amigos* and knowing how deprived the general populace was.

Outside the sea splashed over the wall of the *Malecon,* illegal cab drivers hustled you, and out of nowhere lovely young ladies *(putas)* appeared to tempt angel Gabriel (my middle name). They represented the oldest profession in the world (I thought it was farming.).

In front of the hotel were *"jineteras,"* young women who wanted t be brought in and extend the evening with bed, breakfast and hopefully some new clothes at the dollar store.

I asked a young university student friend of mine the definition and difference between a *puta* and a *jinetera*. He explained *putas* will sleep with anyone for an established price and *jineteras* only sleep with foreigners. They expected to be wined and dined, the next day cash for the night's pleasure, a little shopping, taxi fare and a little extra for their families.

In spite of Castro's Communism and Socialism, the free market system had invaded.

I had moved back to a former residence across from the *Havana Libre* Hotel. It was an apartment building with an elevator that was as tricky as the economy. My landlady was Luisa, a podiatrist who mothered me with care and affection. She had an enormous behind that caused her to waddle, her hair was a bluish platinum, and her lips were always dark red.

When the hot water failed she boiled some for my bath. Often there were patients stretched out with a sheet over them, their bare feet exposed. Felix, her son, was a salsa singer and spoke some English. He acted as interpreter when my girlfriends called. The room had shuttered windows onto a courtyard. There were so many noises in the building I would lie in bed trying to dissect them until they all blurred into one and I fell asleep.

The room had a revolving ceiling fan, a double bed, regularly changed sheets, a daily thermos of ice water and a private entrance, all for $15 a day. In the morning I would go down to Marielo's apartment, a small woman with large eyes, golden skin and a trim figure. She had deep dimples that were very seductive. Her daughter was taller and darker, with almond shaped eyes that searched you and found everything out in seconds. Her long, black oily hair cascaded to her waist and you could not help but imagine her naked under a palm tree. Marielo had been a dancer and showed me photographs of herself in elaborate costumes with most of her well-formed body exposed. She prepared fresh bananas, papaya, pineapple, guava, a small roll and hot strong coffee and steamed milk, all for two dollars. I always got to kiss both cheeks, what an incredible bargain.

Once on the street you were hustled for taxis, black market cigars and rum. Rarely were you asked if you wanted a woman. They seemed to operate independently. When I felt annoyed and was in a hurry I would reply in a joke accent and say I was from Russia, Romania or Hungary, which put an end to the hustling.

One afternoon I went to visit my friend "Chocolate," a dancer rehearsing for the opera Carmen. It took place in a beautiful old building. It was fascinating to watch the lithesome dancers exercise and interact with one another.

Chocolate did a solo part that was passionate and erotic and made my muscles ache to watch. One of her girlfriends who spoke English was introduced and told me how important it was for a young woman to have decent clothes and would I be so kind as to purchase a dress for "Chocolate." I returned a compassionate and caring look and said I would consider the idea. The next day I was invited by my friend called "China" — I had met him on a previous trip — to have lunch at his girlfriend's house in old Havana. The family was very cordial and prepared a beautiful lunch. That evening we went to Carnival on the *Prado.*

It reminded me of Carnival in Rio and Trinidad. The streets were packed with exuberant festive Cubans drinking beer and rum from makeshift containers, always sharing. Beautiful women were everywhere, flashing seductive smiles. I spoke to a beautiful woman who wanted to come along with a friend but China, after interrogating them, felt they were not trustworthy, so I took his advice and sadly left them. Another beautiful senorita approached me and did a very wild dance for me, then started rubbing her body against mine and soon we had a group of admirers applauding. She kissed me and disappeared into the crowd.

The parade was filled with African-costumed women, men and children doing frenzied dances and you wondered where they got the energy with such inadequate diets.

The next day I was slightly frayed, but one rebounds quickly in Havana. The abundance of good looking women is a happy distraction.

Silvia and Oscar invited me on a bus trip to *Cojimar,* where Hemmingway got his inspiration for "The Old Man and the Sea."

It was Sunday. A half hour wait for a bus is nothing. One to two hours is more the norm on weekdays. Silvia paid in pesos; it was all quite drab, the streets were very dirty. We stopped at a development that was built for the Olympics.

Oscar's brother lived there with his wife and two children. He had helped to build the building as part of a cooperative. It was Oscar's brother's birthday and his father was visiting, so we had cake and I was offered rum but I only took a sip as a birthday toast. The apartment was very sparse, but comfortable and clean. They were very proud of their home and few possessions and were extremely warm and hospitable toward me.

Oscar's brother was an engineer and his wife repaired computers. As we left they all gathered on their small balcony, and as we turned to wave goodbye I photographed them.

In *Cojimar* we stopped at the *La Terraza* restaurant, a beautiful old bar with polished wood that Hemmingway frequented, but we didn't stay. It was overpriced and crowded with a bus load of German tourists. The village is very run down with no special charm. We stopped on a small footpath bridge across a canal leading to a small marina. A man was fishing for crabs with a small cage filled with fish parts. Oscar made arrangements with him to buy fish for our lunch later in the week.

We stopped by Gregoria Fuente's house but he was not home. He was Hemmingway's fishing guide and skipper and gave him inspiration for *"The Old Man and the Sea."* There was a longer wait for a return bus. This time it was one of those cavernous disjointed contraptions that were joined in the middle and wiggled as we rode along. There were holes in the ceiling that Silvia felt obliged to apologize for. Everyone looked at me curiously, everyone looked tired and drained. It was like riding in the belly of a dinosaur.

Silvia and Oscar are my dearest friends. Oscar and I cannot converse because of the language barrier but our feelings overcome the impasse so we laugh and hug one another.

Oscar's high-ceilinged apartment is filled with his artwork of clever constructions of Havana street scenes. He has given me several and he made one for my daughter, Josephine. Silvia made one for my son, Nevin. Silvia also gave them cassettes of her songs.

Oscar is an excellent cook and I know they used their monthly rations on me — and sure enough, fresh fish from *Cojimar.* Oscar's other brother is a sculptor and looks like a young Harpo Marx. He is in his thirties with a powerful build. He was wearing a small fedora with blond curls nearly touching his shoulder. He had a beautiful smile and spoke half Spanish and half English very rapidly, he was so eager to communicate

He did quick pencil sketches of me while he talked and I ate. They were flattering but I looked too youthful, I felt.

It suddenly turned cold, Havana had a record cold temperature. Even I was cold, not having brought sufficient clothing. Silvia arrived in layers like an expensive cake describing each layer of clothing. She held a handkerchief to a constantly dripping nose. It prompted me to decide on a trip south to *Santiago, Baracoa* and possibly *Gibara* on the south coast.

While purchasing my ticket at Havana Tours it was suggested I could get a car and driver for three days for the price of $132, which included a meal each day. The cost of the translator was five dollars a day. I hate tours but since I was to be alone it appealed to me. And the price was right.

The flight was on time and only took an hour. My driver, Pedro, who met me at the airport, was a young man with a mustache and slightly balding. He was way overweight, which he joked about and constantly alluded to.

Rafael, my translator, was a trained university student who didn't get enough to eat. His wardrobe consisted of a few tee shirts and a coule of pairs of socks.

As the days went on Rafael expressed his anger and frustration. He lived on 15 pesos a week, less than a dollar. He was married with a child. His wife and child were in Guantanamo.

He stayed at the university and shared his room with a girlfriend. He was studying English and would be graduating this year, then on to teaching. He felt Castro had betrayed them by turning to Communism. He said he would leave his wife and child if he could escape to the states .and make a lot of money, his prime goal. It was obvious he watched too many American movies.

I was very hungry and suggested lunch and asked about *paladars.* Pedro took me to a home that was orderly and spotlessly clean. An attractive young girl was our waitress, so we were all happy. Pedro got nervous and explained I was only allowed $3 toward my meal and they would wait in the car. I invited them to lunch and bought them a couple of beers.

He took me to a family home where I had a room with a private entrance and a beautiful vegetable garden opposite me in the suburbs. The owner spoke a little English, the whole family was utterly charming and could not do enough for me for $12 a night. He was an engineer and his wife was a dentist. Before they left for work in the morning they left a tray with hot coffee and milk, fresh bread and a tortilla and an assortment of fresh fruit, all for $2.

Before I left they found out from Rafael that I had written several books and they elevated me to patron saint. We drove into downtown Santiago, which captivated me. The streets were narrow and clogged with people on foot. There were few modern buildings. There were beautiful churches, old government buildings and clean parks that were full of people and the plazas were the meeting place for everyone. When we walked the streets we encountered many beautiful women who were friendly and flirtatious.

Santiago is the second largest city in Cuba, with a population of 400,000. It is not nearly as run down as Havana. The colonial architecture, combined with balconies, latticework and wrought iron gates, gave it a lazy, sensuous atmosphere. Surrounding the city's tiled roof buildings were lovely rolling slopes covered with sugar cane and coffee plantations.

I had heard and read about *Casa de la Trova*, where the local peasant singers performed, and wanted very much to ex-

perience it. We arrived later in the afternoon. People were clinging to the grill work to peek in at the performers. We walked in
through massive doors into an 18th-century building. It cost me
$2. Pedro and Rafael used pesos. The main room was filled
with paintings and photographs of musicians. Rows of chairs
covered with cowhide were neatly lined. I was the only foreigner
present. The women smiled openly; women are not coy in Cuba.

The music was passionate, small groups with several guitars, maracas, clavas, bongos, and everyone sang. Many of the
instruments were patched together. At night the musicians performed in the courtyard, which was very romantic, where there
was room to dance among the tables and you could purchase
drinks. The music was very intense. The next day we went to
the *Moncada* garrison, where Castro failed in an assault in 1953.
It was also there that Castro accepted the surrender of Batista's
army in 1959. It had been turned into a simple museum with all
the bullet holes intact. We visited Ifigenia Cemetery, once seg-
regated by race and racial class, full of large mausoleums and
the tomb of Cuban patriot Jose Marti. It is sculpted with six
shields so that it always lies in the sun.

There was always a bottle of rum in the car that Rafael and
Pedro took long swigs on. At lunch they had several beers, but
they never got drunk; we had many laughs. The conversation
centered on women and the economy. The main mode of transportation in the suburbs was horse-drawn carts that seated twenty
or thirty people with a makeshift canopy to protect them from
the fierce summer sun.

One of the sights on my agenda was to visit a folkloric
groups in rehearsal called *"Cutumba."* This was based on African and Haitian heritage. The Africans were from slaves brought
here by the Spaniards to work the canefields and the Haitians
(both black and white) who settled after escaping the slave up-
risings of their country in 1700, bringing with them the French
characteristics of their culture. Pedro, Rafael and I walked up
creaking stairs after much difficulty in locating the building.

A small group of musicians was practicing while the dancers drank and bathed their faces during a break from a faucet on

the balcony.

They were all unbelievably beautiful and handsome, sweating and basking in the sunshine. I asked permission to photograph them and they were delighted. Maritza, an elegant, dusky dancer with a slender body, long neck and slanted eyes, spoke bits of English and pinched me after I photographed her. I was startled but kept cool, so I asked Rafael what it all meant. He spoke to her and said she likes you, so I arranged to meet her for dinner that night.

What happened after that was too romantic to describe and I was deeply touched by her sincerity and unaffected charm. I took a letter back to be mailed to her brother in New Jersey and called, but his phone had been disconnected. The following day we drove out to the *Basilica of El Cobre*, the most sacred shrine of the Virgin in Cuba, where worshipers flock to be healed and leave their crutches.

It is perched in the foothills of the *Sierra Maestra*, the holiest of holies. Its cream-colored structure with red domes surrounded by royal palms and lush vegetation would make a believer of anyone.

When we arrived at the parking lot we were descended upon by hordes of zealous hustlers pushing minerals into our hands and religious cards describing the church. One was fiercer than the other and they refused to take back the offered minerals.

The church was impressive and cool. When we left we were pounced upon again like flies on rotting meat. We had to drive cautiously for fear of running them over.

We drove down the highway and stopped at a small farmhouse that had been turned into a museum. It was where Castro and the Che Guevara rendezvoused for an attack on the *Mancada* Garrison. There were white marble stones placed at intervals along the highway as shrines with the names of the patriots killed in the attack.

We continued south along a smooth highway rumored to be used as a landing strip in case of an invasion by U.S. planes. On our way to *Baconoa* we passed a park with life-size dinosaurs, with the mountains as a backdrop. The glimpse was very compelling but I was anxious to get to the freshwater lake ahead.

All the large, elaborate government hotels on the coast appeared to be empty. There was a sign for an aquarium ahead, and loving fish as I do I asked to stop. Pedro and Rafael pulled out the rum bottle took long drinks and argued. A young woman in the parking lot offered her services but we all politely declined.

The marine show was in progress, with roughly fifteen people in the audience. There were two black seals catching balls, barking, rolling over and playing dead until they were rewarded with small fish. Dolphins made spectacular leaps. When the show ended an attendant asked if we would like to get into a pool with dolphins for $7. I immediately took him up and offered to pay for Pedro and Rafael, who were terrified by the prospect. I changed into my swimsuit and was guided over to a small pool. The dolphins' trainer was a young attractive girl wearing no bra, who held the close attention of Pedro and Rafael.

There were two dolphins in the pool and she explained through Rafael how I should behave. She knew what to expect from the dolphins.

I slipped into the pool and she told me to tread water. When she blew her whistle the dolphins would swim past me at a furious speed and I was to grab there dorsal fins. The whistle blew and they came charging from behind. I grabbed their fins and held on, hoping I wouldn't have a stroke. They pulled me like two torpedoes, leaving a foaming wake behind. We did that several times. My heart was pumping, I was thrilled and exhausted. Next I floated on the surface and she had them jump over me, twenty feet out of the water. I thought, if they came crashing down on me I'm done for. I gave Rafael my camera so he was snapping pictures of the whole event. Pedro and the trainer were howling. She had the Dolphins roll over on their backs and I hugged them and stroked their stomachs, which felt like highly polished leather.

I got out of the pool. The dolphins came to the side and she told me to touch their heads and then touch my cheek. They both stood on their tails and pressed their heads against my face as if they were kissing me, chattering, clicking and clacking, giving a wide grin the whole time. For that they were given several handfuls of fish. I was trembling with excitement and felt physically exhilarated. The trainer gave me a kiss as a reward.

The persistent woman was still in the parking lot; she made us another offer at a lower price. We drove down to a beautiful freshwater lake next to the ocean, it was quite unbelievable. We had a good lunch. I dined on small fish from the lake served by beautiful friendly waitresses. Pedro and Rafael had five or six beers each and were able to pay for their food in pesos. Normally they would not even be allowed to dine there.

We spoke to a fisherman on the lake in a government boat and through Rafael I was able to get some information. There were large fish in the lake. There was a channel from the lake into the sea. The fisherman said the dolphins would swim in from the sea and dine on the freshwater fish.

When I got excited he said he would take me fishing in the lake, which was a couple of miles long, and also in the sea and I could stay in his house. It was tempting, but I said I would come back another time. A young man was feeding crocodiles in a pen. The largest looked well over ten feet long. Their submarine periscopic eyes seemed to float on the surface. To entertain us he got in the pen with a 20-foot pole and prodded them. They responded by lunging and snapping their cavernous manytoothed snouts. Standing 100 feet away it sent a chill through me, although I have seen many in the wild in South America. He told us they were all taken from the lake and local swamps.

It was time to move on. Pedro took me to the airlines office to purchase a ticket to Baracoa. It cost $17 for a half-hour flight. I had several contacts through my friend Silvia in Havana.

The flight was on schedule we touched down at noon on a bright day. Baracoa is on the south coast, so we flew in over the ocean. The cluster of ancient buildings aroused a sense of adventure.

There had been a terrible storm two days before, so the

inhabitants were coping with it. A taxi driver approached me speaking rapidly in Spanish, which did neither of us any good. Some handsome young teenagers who spoke some English came to the rescue and claimed my bags.

Outside the terminal small children gathered around me and knew a few words of English. They were beautiful. Although they didn't beg I gave them some coins. Their good-natured simplicity revived me and put me in a happy mood. Because of the recent storm there had been a landslide and the airport road had been washed out. One of the teenagers lifted my heavy suitcase onto his shoulder and we trudged through red muck and boulders while earth removing equipment worked down below to clear the road. My driver's car, a relic, was parked just beyond the mud line. I said I was hungry so I was taken to a *paladar* and I shared lunch and bought drinks for my companions.

Baracoa is the oldest city in Cuba, which was discovered by Columbus in 1492. Little had changed, it seemed. The buildings were rickety the streets narrow; there were few cars. The city itself was founded by Diego Velazques, a conquistador from Spain, in 1510, "the Americas' oldest town."

After lunch I was taken to the *La Rusa* hotel, founded by a Russian woman who left the Soviet Union in the '50s and joined the Cuban rebels. Both Fidel and Che had stayed there. They had no rooms and could not change a $10 bill. There were two new ugly governments hotels which did not appeal to me, so my new-found friends took me down the street to the Delfino family.

Everything was hush-hush because of the police, so I paid the taxi drivers indoors and made arrangements for my lodging. I had a private spacious rom, both simple and clean, for $12, with meals arranged. I bonded immediately with the Delfinos. The grandmother, "Dulce," adopted me, her husband never left my side. Their daughter and son-in-law and their two children were all introduced. They squeezed me fresh orange juice and brought over a neighbor named John, a strapping young man in his early thirties who spoke good English.

After I unpacked I wandered around the town and became

a local curio. It was very poor but fascinating, a surviving antiquity. Everything was crumbling and ancient. Although charming to me, I surmised how the residents were struggling.

In the main square stood the *Nuestra Senora de la Asuncion* church built in 1805, where the cross of the *Parra* was kept, which was brought by Columbus from Spain. It was kept in a glass case. The curator looked as old as the cross and I felt obliged to photograph them together. I labored up the steps to the *El Castillo* hotel overlooking the city to cash some travelers checks.

There were some prosperous-looking tourists laughing at the pool, drinking and smoking cigars, and I couldn't wait to get back to the Delfinos. I wandered into the airline office, which had a tawdry facade, and a young man spoke to me in English and startled me. His name was Max. To my dismay I found out there was only one flight a week to Santiago and no transportation to *Gibara* up the coast, which I had planned on visiting.

He suggested staying at a small hotel out of town on the beach once he learned I liked to fish.

Max took me to the house of a taxi driver and we made arrangements for transportation the next day, all done through a small window from the street. The building looked as though it was going to collapse. That evening John came by after dinner and asked if I wanted to go to *La Trova,* a smaller an more primitive version of what I had witnessed in Santiago.

John was desperate to escape. He was an engineer and made the equivalent of four dollars a month. There were no lights in the narrow back streets. John guided me across gutters and potholes and pushed me aside as a bicycle swished by.

It was after 9 p.m. and *La Trova* was already jumping. The street outside was packed with laughing half-drunk revelers. Inside the musicians were strumming their guitars and singing. A small floor was crowded with dancers.

Several of John's friends, very drunk, took an interest in me. I gave John money to buy rum which we shared with everyone within reach. An incredibly beautiful young gypsy-like girl danced in front of me and kept tugging at me to join her. I still had not recovered from Maritza in Santiago, so I deferred and I will regret it to this day.

The next day I met my taxi driver, Miguel, and headed for the beach. I told Max to come out two days later with his family and join me for lunch and then I would take the taxi over the mountains back to Santiago. It was a beautiful ride out crossing rivers lush with vegetation. I had him stop at a coconut plantation with hundreds of young nuts sprouting so I could photograph it.

We arrived at the hotel after chugging along in his red hand-painted 1960 Zephyr from England. The hotel was directly on the beach and I was the only guest. The cook was an attractive woman and she, the driver and I discussed the menu as best we could.

My room faced the sea. It was government-owned and cost $25 per night. The cook's daughter, who was nine or ten years old, came out. She was totally charming, dark with large curious eyes and playful. We became immediate friends. I thought of my own daughter, Josephine, at that age, and suddenly felt very lonely. My son, Nevin, gave me two books for my birthday. One, *Running in the Family* by Michael Ondaatje, was about Sri Lanka and made me think of my two sister Buddhist friends, Beeta and Mala, from back home, who were from Sri Lanka.

He also had written me a beautiful poem and I began to realize how far away he was and how much I loved him. I felt very sentimental. After I started reading I calmed down. Some Italian tourists arrived for lunch who I recognized from *La Trova* the previous night. I put my collapsible fishing pole together and walked over to a cliff jutting out into the sea. Out of nowhere several young boys showed up and started catching small crabs among the rocks and breaking open periwinkles for bait, but I had no luck.

They gave me some sweet bananas and suggested lunch in a shack near the beach for $5. Two hours later lunch was announced. It turned out to be delicious, fresh fish cooked in a mild sauce, fried bananas and rice, salad and fresh fruit. Several boys lined up on a bench and watched me eat. I took two of them back to the hotel and bought them a beer.

On the way back a young couple approached us, a white girl in a sarong spoke to me. She was French and complained about the country, the transportation problems and the Cuban women. It was midday and hot so I just listened. Her boyfriend said only a few words and we parted.

I took a nap then tried to make fishing arrangements, with no luck. The cook's daughter returned from school with a lovely friend and we went for a walk together. The sea was calm so I went for a swim and read some more. Someone kept turning on the cassette player and I kept turning it off.

Dinnertime arrived and I got Cokes from the kitchen. They had no ice and I poured a stiff rum from the bottle I had with me. I offered the cook a drink, which she accepted, and we drank in silence. Her daughter and friend shared a Coke.

I went into the empty dining room and sat down. The cook came out and nodded. A half hour later she came out with a plate with a small portion of white rice and a slice of pork. That was all they had. After dinner I had a cup of strong lukewarm coffee and my cigar.

The hotel manager, a young black man, strolled into the dining room and I invited him to join me. I thought to myself, "I had better get my intentions across emphatically." First I bought him a pack of cigarettes and a Coke and kept saying taxi, *manana*. He understood. There was no telephone so he had to go a long distance by bicycle in the morning to call a taxi from town.

Breakfast was an egg, dry bread and coffee. I was packed by 8 a.m. At 10 a.m. a 1940s Willy's Jeep arrived with driver and the manager. I said goodbye to the cook and kissed her daughter. The driver took me to a *paladar* in town that was very good. I had beef for the first time. I treated him to lunch and he went out and got a bottle of rum, which we shared with the owner.

Of course I went back to the Delfinos, who were surprised to see me. I got hold of John and he said he would get me on a bus the next day to Santiago.

I found out where Max lived and left word with his wife. It was obvious I would not be out at the beach on Sunday.

That night it was the *La Trova* again. The same drunks

swarmed over me but the gypsy girl was missing.

The next day, after getting my early morning kiss and embrace from Dulce, I packed, strolled the streets photographing, had lunch, and went to the bus station with John at noon. The bus left at 2 p.m. I gave John $9 for the fare and a $3 bribe. From the bench inside the terminal I could se *El Yunque*, a high square mountain that looks like an island or more like the haircut young rap singers are wearing these days.

After I saw the last passenger climb aboard and the bus leave with a friend of mine from the hotel on it, John returned with a hang dogged look full of apologies.

Senor Delfino had come to see me off on his bicycle, he also seemed embarrassed. We piled back into the taxi and I was greeted warmly by the remaining Delfinos. *La Trova* was getting less interesting. The next day John admitted shamefacedly he could not get me on the bus.

I said "get me a taxi," a line my son Nevin used when he was around ten years old at the play "The Wizard" in New York, which scared hell out of him.

It turned out to be the same 1960 red Zephyr that had taken me to the beach. It needed some repairs so I went with John and friends to a river, fished and swam to kill some time.

The red Zephyr rolled around about 2:30 p.m. The Delfinos gathered around for another goodbye, we were all laughing. John decided to go along and Miguel substituted his brother, Tomas, and off we sped. Not really, the car showed little enthusiasm for speed.

The trip was calculated at five hours. Once in the mountains it became cool. The highway was in good condition and there was little traffic. Huge open trucks would pass us crammed with standing passengers like cattle. John said there were many fatalities.

The old Zephyr conked out. Tomas, nonplussed, dug into its innards and soon had it rumbling again.

We climbed slowly to the top of the mountain range. The scenery became more spectacular. Deep gorges and ribbon-like rivers snaked their ways through canyon walls. Wisps of smoke drifted up from hidden villages.

The old Zephyr gasped again and sputtered to a stop. Tomas behaved like a doctor on emergency. With a cigarette dangling from his lips he disappeared under the hood and soon his patient coughed, gagged and resumed a desperate cadence. Off we crawled upward.

By the time we reached Guantanamo it was 5 p.m. A very dirty-looking street vendor was selling pork sandwiches and I declined John's offer to join them and pulled out a banana from several I had saved as a gift from John the day before. Tomas was a chain smoker and John, who confided in me wanted to be a professional swimmer, avoided the stuff. We stopped to get directions for a bypass to Santiago. From the quantities of cigarettes Tomas had smoked, I was sure *he* needed a bypass. Dusk was taking over as we passed an enormous freshwater lake that was the water supply for Guantanamo.

The roads were poorly marked so we kept backtracking. Suddenly I got the bright idea to return to Bacanao and meet up with the fisherman and spend a few days there. The friendly and attractive waitresses at the lake restaurant became a fantasy wanting to be realized. Tomas was agreeable for an extra $10, which I was comfortable with, knowing it was way out of the way.

It was 8:30 p.m. when we arrived in Bacanao. There were no street lights and very few buildings had lights. I tried to guide them from memory but it was impossible to distinguish the landmarks in the dark.

We arrived at a military barrier and they sent us off in another direction. A group of men clustered around a lantern said it was the only hotel and the restaurant I had in mind was closed. It did not look the least bit inviting and no one spoke English, so I said, "Let's head for Santiago."

The Delfino family had given me the address of their son, Dr. Pedro Lobaina Delfino. No sooner had we left and the car broke down again. Tomas dismantled the carburetor, blew and sucked on the lines, intermittently puffing on his cigarette. I was expecting a conflagration. It worked for a kilometer or two and then the engine died. My suitcase had to be removed form the trunk to get at more tools. Tomas had an emergency light that he hooked up to the battery under the hood. I had to give him credit, he was prepared. John acted as a surgeon's assistant, handing tools to Tomas and placing the small parts in organized piles in the dark. I offered to help by staying out of the way. We were barely off the road and gigantic buses, trucks and passengers cars whizzed by us at breakneck speed, veering suddenly to avoid us. It raised what little hair I had left on the back of my head. Consequently it was a litany of breakdowns with repeated mechanical efforts and never once did Tomas lose his cool, for which I praised him.

Reaching Santiago that night was out of the question. I kept falling asleep in the back seat; it turned cold. I curled up into a fetal position and longed for my mother's womb.

I awoke at dawn as Tomas and John had just finished another major operation and the car purred like a well-fed kitten. School children lined the highway waiting for buses. We were all in a confident mood, laughing, when the right front wheel fell off.

When that was put back on we limped into Santiago at 9 a.m., eighteen-and-a-half hours later. Pedro Delfino had been expecting us. His mother had called and he had not left for work. He was a handsome and robust gentleman. He introduced me to his attractive and charming wife, Marlin, who insisted on feeding me. hey lived on the top floor of an old building. Pigs grunted on their terrace and I was shown to my room up a winding iron stairs similar to one I had in my apartment in New York, overlooking the city. I took a hot shower and fell into bed with a fan oscillating with a quiet drone. Several hours later Marlin prepared a light lunch and I met their teenage son, Edwin.

I strolled around the city and struck up numerous conversations. A young woman in an art gallery invited me to lunch the next day and I thought of Maritza, but time was running out.

I had dinner and heard the news of two American planes having been shot down. We heard a news report on TV which kept getting blacked out, which Pedro blamed on the United States. Pedro was very calm about the incident and I began to wonder how it might affect me, since I had another week to spend in Cuba.

The next day I left for Havana. In front of me was a very beautiful girl. I asked the agent to put her next to me. It turned out she spoke some English. We met again in the waiting area and she asked if we could share a taxi in Havana and I was more than willing to oblige.

On our way home from the airport into Havana she told me she was a model. She was well dressed and had expensive luggage. Silvia had informed me any woman with luxury items was highly suspect.

I dropped her off at her residence in the suburbs and she agreed to meet me for dinner. It never happened. There were no English language newspapers available in Havana. On my last trip I was able to get an *International Herald Tribune*. I tried all the major hotels and ended up with a weekly English copy of the government newspaper. The account of course denounced America for allowing the "Brothers for Peace" to continually trespass on Cuban air space. That afternoon I decided on a rooftop swim at the Hotel Capri, which was almost spitting distance from the Hotel Nacional.

While swimming I heard an American voice on a cellular phone. A middle-aged man with two small children was carrying on a conversation about the protest that was expected because of the shooting incident.

Not wanting to eavesdrop I swam out of earshot. When he was finished I introduced myself. His name was Frank. He was a freelance American journalist living in Cuba. He had been talking to other international journalists who were waiting for a news break.

I told Frank it reminded me of Key West when I lived there and Harry Truman came down and the journalists followed him, hungry for news. Frank said the whole thing was a fiasco and the embargo was an international embarrassment and Clinton couldn't be trusted to make a decision and stick to it. He put me at ease and he proved to be right.

A group of guitar players and singers started to perform. A

middle-aged couple began dancing and they were as smooth as whipped cream. A young girl joined the group and began singing. She looked to be in her teens, with long fake silver fingernails, and she sang with deep mature passion. I thought of the young bullfighter in Hemmingway's *The Sun Also Rises*.

When she finished singing I complimented the whole group. It turned out her father and brother were two of the three guitar players.

When I got back to my room I found that both Nevin and Josephine had been trying to reach me. After many calls we finally hooked up and I was very nonchalant and said "what incident." When the joke was over I assured them all was calm and I was absolutely safe. We had a good laugh and they were relieved. That evening we went to the *Gran Teatro* in old Havana, a building as old and ornate as Spanish lace. We met Cristo, Silvia's son, who is an opera singer in the current production of Carmen. Oscar purchased me a ticket in pesos, so I kept my mouth shut as we entered.

There were tiers of balconies and only a scattering of patrons. It was a skimpy program of opera excerpts. After the performance I was introduced to some of Cristo's friends. One in particular, a beautiful pianist, flirted with me.

The next afternoon we went to old Havana to purchase black market cigars from a beautiful friend of Silvia's. $30 for a box of 25, Cuba's best and Fidel's favorite, *Cohibas*.

We stopped by to hear and photograph *Grupo "Piel Morena,"* six beautiful and talented female musicians. They were rehearsing upstairs in a lovely old building. They played, danced and sang, ranging in color from ebony to coffee and cream, one more exotic than the other.

It was impossible not to fall in love with all of them; their beauty, smiles, movements, were intoxicating. I took several rolls of film, joking and flirting for a couple of hours. When they finished rehearsing they took their bicycles (which they kept upstairs for safe keeping) and went home.

Next we went to see my friend Lazaro Valdez, who was rehearsing with his group, Bamboleo. They were rehearsing in the courtyard of a beautiful old home. Most everyone had arrived on bicycles. In between songs Lazaro embraced me and inquired about my love life. He vowed to find me a suitable companion when I returned.

Knowing the group I was greeted with hugs and smiles. Silvia sat on the sidelines sniffing into a soggy handkerchief with a terrible cold while I shot several rolls of film

We left among warm goodbyes and embraces ,promising each other to stay in touch.

My last night was planned to spend at the Dos Gardenias nightclub to hear my friend Ela Calvo sing. After a late dinner of leftovers at Oscar's we left for the club. She didn't start singing until 11 p.m. Ela, a large black woman, greeted me like an old friend, with strong embraces and kisses. She smelled like a bouquet of gardenias. She thanked me for the many photographs of her I had sent. She was turning one into a poster.

There were a number of female and male singers performing, all competent, and rewarded with hushed attention and strong applause. When Ela sang the audience was transported like a religious cult. She sang of unrequited love as though she had experienced every sad lyric herself. .One could not help but feel the pain of lost romances.

She joined us at our table and held my hand and said she would miss me and look forward to my next visit. It was all the more poignant with Silvia translating. I felt very sad. We kissed and said goodbye as a singer poured his heart out in the background.

Arrangements had been made for a taxi the next morning. Another "Tomas." His taxi had broken down so he had a friend take me and he came along for the ride.

Women were the topic as the three of us pointed out lovely examples of Havana offerings along the way. Silvia and Oscar met me at the airport so I had a tempestuous, loving and tearful farewell. Arriving in Nassau, I had just the right amount of time to claim my bag, purchase a bottle of rum and scotch at the duty free shop, and head for U.S. Customs.

It so happened a woman agent flagged me and asked me

where I had spent my time and I said "Nassau," knowing my passport had not been stamped in Cuba. To my surprise she asked me to open my suitcase. The few Cuban cigars and gifts were evidence of my embarkment. She asked me how long I had been in Cuba so as not to further embroil myself I said, "30 days." She had me remove most of the contents and methodically rifled through my belonging.

She set aside the cigars and a few objects with Cuba stamped on them, and then proceeded to take hand-made craft items I had purchased for Nevin, Josephine and friends. In a subtle tone I asked if that were necessary. She obviously was embarrassed and mumbled it was her duty. I remarked what an unpleasant job she had and she agreed.

She placed the items in a pile and said they would be destroyed. She filled out an official form listing the objects and had me sign it. Knowing that I had gone to Cuba illegally I thought it best not to challenge her. She said I could have gotten official permission as a writer, but I said the red tape involved would have taken too long and she agreed.

Feeling contrite she left a few gifts, gave me a weak smile, and waved me on.

At my change of planes in Charlotte, North Carolina I got into a conversation with a pleasant couple from Black Lake, New York. As we were boarding I said, "Have a safe trip, I'm on it." Heading off ino freezing temperatures I thought of all my wonderful hot blooded friends I was leaving behind.

Costa Rica

My wife, Alison, announced she was going to house sit up in the mountains near my daughter Josephine's school in Putney, Vermont. The idea did not appeal to me since it wasn't on a lake, so my mind began to whir and I opted for a solitary sojourn to Costa Rica.

Josephine had been there the previous summer. We had enrolled her in a program helping poor families — the cost put us at a disadvantage as well. Josephine loved the whole experience, but when I attempted to enroll her in a Quaker school up in the mountains of Monteverde, where they had no phones, the appeal quickly evaporated and she declined my offer.

Alison decided to fly down and join Josephine for a week. she came back with the impression it was the New Zealand (where we had once lived) of the Caribbean: not much culture and bland food.

My passion is fishing, which is one of many things Costa Rica is famous for, so I had to see for myself. On a trip to the Azores several years ago I had hired a boat to go fishing for blue marlin. I must confess I am not a big game fisherman and I have a weak stomach and unsteady sea legs. Alison was wise enough to refuse the invitation, but I felt my son, Nevin, and Josephine should have the experience. Josephine was 13 and Nevin 15.

Our skipper was Rick Ruhlow and he told us a 1,146-pound blue marlin had been boated from Horta Faial. Rick was young and personable. Alison waved us off into choppy seas. White-caps greeted us with a vengeance when we hit the open waters of the Atlantic. both Nevin and Josephine turned a slime green and lost several days of exotic food.

I felt as badly as they did but miraculously held down my stomach contents. In these conditions we had to turn around. It was a costly expedition but I couldn't torture them further. We dropped them off, pale and subdued (it did have some benefits), and Rick suggested fishing another area for lack of time.

My stomach fibrillates just thinking of the experience. My macho persona would not allow me to admit defeat, plus the big bucks invested. We didn't raise a fish and secretly I didn't care; I was unsteady for days after.

After making Rick's acquaintance I found out his father, Jerry, was a journalist for the Tico Times in Costa Rica. When I returned to my home in Clinton, New York I began corresponding with his father, who wrote mainly articles on fishing.

Each time I had planned a trip to Costa Rica, something intervened. The last time was an invitation to Uruguay by the Uruguayan Tourist Board to write about the country. But the time arrived and I was excited, having read a lot of literature about Costa Rica and in particular, fishing.

After several phone calls to Jerry I asked if there was anything I could bring, and he almost sobbed into the phone: pastrami, corned beef, pumpernickel bread, deli food — I promised to fulfill his desires.

I bought a small Coleman ice chest and filled it to the brim. Jerry lived out in the suburbs of Santa Ana; he thought it best to meet me at the airport. He had recently broken his leg on a fishing expedition fishing for guapote in a remote area. I later fished for these strong fighters in a more subdued setting, Lake Arenal. Jerry was wearing a cast and on crutches — I jokingly told him to wear a red carnation.

My plane touched down in a warm tropical drizzle. The rush of exotic fragrances greeted my nostrils, the dark Latins flashed smiles, and I felt at ease. Money changers with great wads of bills between their fingers and carrying calculators approached me, but I waved them off.

I went into an area where passengers were being greeted emotionally by family and friends and for a moment I felt lonely. Taxi drivers asked if I needed transportation. Most spoke English, and throughout the trip no one hassled me like they would in Mexico and other Latin tourist-oriented destinations.

About twenty minutes later I spotted Jerry on crutches with two friends, both named Timothy. Jerry had seen photographs of me on my book jackets, but I had the upper hand in recognition.

After introductions we headed into the rain. Tim Britton was an American — a doctor practicing in Costa Rica — and Tim Hodgson, an Englishman, was part owner of Hotel Del Rey, a new hotel in downtown San Jose. They made me feel like I was an old friend. We stopped by a liquor store for some seven-year-old Nicaraguan rum that turned out to be as good as the praises.

We were greeted at Jerry's home by Celia, Jerry's mate, a sensuous and charming woman of African and French descent. Alex, her fair-skinned 12-year-old son, spoke to me in perfect English and we bonded immediately. We settled into rum and Cokes with fresh limes from their tree, while a small parrot chattered.

I felt at home with Celia's warm hospitality and Alex's wide grin. The two Tims patiently answered my many questions and Jerry and I felt we knew one another through our exchange of letters. Jerry invited the two Tims back to share in the deli feast, the next day being Father's Day.

I was shown to a quiet back bedroom and fell asleep immediately with a cool soft breeze playing over my body.

Being an early riser and a light sleeper I heard the roosters crow; it was 7 a.m. The house was silent. I dressed and took to the street. It was a middle class neighborhood that did not look very foreign except for the vegetation and Spanish signs. A lone man passed me on a bicycle and I hailed him in fluent Spanish: "Hola! Buenos dias!" (one of the few phrases I know.) I then asked in English if he knew of a restaurant. He answered in perfect English; he was American. He was going to Soda Ricky's (soda is a term for all snack bars and small restaurants). He gave me directions and I caught up with him.

(Since all of my notes were lost in an incident I shall explain later, I cannot give my newfound friend's name. All details will be from memory.)

He had a small business growing trees, shrubbery and decorative plants for landscaping. I ordered a typical breakfast of fresh orange juice, rice and beans with scrambled eggs, toast and hot milk and coffee. The coffee is not nearly as good as you would expect from a country that grows it. My best cup of coffee ever — and I have had it all over the world — was in the Miami airport. It was a tiny cup of Cuban coffee with a rich froth made with Bustello coffee, a brand that I used in my former restaurant, Martell's, in New York City.

Three middle-aged women fussed over me as I learned my new friend was also from Upstate New York, where I live now. It was a delicious breakfast for a very modest price. When I returned home the family was up and protested politely that I hadn't eaten at home.

I asked Alex what he would like to do and he suggested taking a taxi to the mall. The mall was very modest other than a well-stocked supermarket. I bought a present for Celia, some weird stretchy clammy play dough for Alex, and gave him money to play Nintendo. We had to call a taxi and waited nearly an hour before returning home.

The next day was Father's Day and I called my best friend, John Zartarian, on his 57th birthday. He was already at work in his restaurant, The Paddock in Hyannis, Massachusetts, on Cape Cod.

That afternoon a young couple visited with their new child, a boy that was only a few months old. He was from Australia and she was from England. They had just taken over an English language newspaper.

Tim Britton showed up with two small children. Celia's affection was without bounds, and she soon was playing fondly with all three children. Tim Hodgson showed up on his way to a date he was quite excited about. Jerry and Celia served a good cold beer called Pilsen and made sandwiches from the cold cuts and we wolfed down the Brie in ecstasy.

Jerry knew I was anxious to go fishing, so he invited over a friend and fishing guide, Peter Gorinsky. Peter was from British Guiana, now Guyana. I had been there two years ago and we shared names of mutual friends, like Diane McTurk, who owned a large ranch and had river otters for pets. Diane had invited me to her ranch but circumstances never allowed. Peter, because of political problems, left the country. Peter had once befriended a river otter pup that grew to nearly six feet. Playful as they are, they can be quite destructive in domestic quarters. He released it back into the wilds and a year later he encountered a group of otters on the river. One broke away from the pack and swam up to him; it was his old friend.

I made arrangements with Peter to go fishing for guapote on Lake Arenal, but not until Wednesday and I was restless, so Jerry suggested a bus trip to Puntarenas on the Gulf of Nicoya. I took a taxi to San Jose to catch the bus. The fare was cheap and the bus clean and comfortable.

It was good to be in the countryside. It took roughly three hours and rained all the way. The hills and valleys were a dark green and white, water gushed down the many chasms we crossed. There was lightning and thunder and I was enjoying the whole spectacle. The driver had a schedule to keep and he drove at a ferocious speed around hair-raising turns. I relaxed, knowing it was routine for him.

We arrived at Puntarenas on the minute, passing run-down homes and litter-scattered streets. The bus station was crowded. I walked over to the seashore, which was full of trash, and felt rather dejected.

I had read about the Yacht Club as a place to stay. A vendor saw my plight and called over a friend, who went to find a taxi for me. I tipped him and drove back down the highway to the Yacht Club.

It was clean and friendly and they found someone to speak English. I took a room with no air conditioning, but on close inspection it was very drab, so I transferred to a room on the water for a dollar more. I had a cold beer overlooking the river and felt a lot better.

My English-speaking friend put me in touch with a skipper of a fishing boat who spoke English, and we agreed on a price for the following day.

The World's Cup soccer matches were in full swing and the Costa Ricans are rabid fans. It was contagious; besides, there was little else to do but stare at the television and listen to their shouts and screams. It was even more fun over the radio; the announcers went mad rolling their R's.

I was down on the dock at 7 a.m. when the skipper pulled alongside in a well-kept 27-foot white boat with outriggers and two 160-horsepower outboard motors. We gassed up, took on a mate and headed down the brown, polluted river crowded with derelict boats, gulls, pelicans and ramshackle waterfront properties.

My skipper was much too brown from the sun. His Scandinavian background showed in his skin pigment and bleached hair.

At the mouth of the river the water swirled in deep, dangerous whirlpools. Soon we were in the clean blue water of the Pacific Ocean. We headed for some giant remnants of volcanic upheavals. They were covered with cormorants, their guano drippings looking like long white bleached beards. The cormorants would leave their rookery when bait appeared on the surface, diving frantically.

The currents were very strong and it was hard to keep the boat steady. Fish showed up on the boat's sonar screen but we couldn't entice them to strike. The skipper was frustrated, but I wasn't bothered by it, the environment was so beautiful and distracting. A large manta ray surfaced near the boat, its black backside glistening, two hornlike appendages protruding, making it look like a spaceship with its broad wing-like structure. Turtles came up and gasped for air and submerged, leaving behind a dimpled swirl.

Dolphin's ran ahead and cavorted, seemingly for our amusement. We trolled as close to the rocks as possible, hoping to catch a rooster fish, but instead I caught a small dolphin fish that was going to be our lunch.

The skipper kept hitting the sonar screen as the largest image of fish it could project swam across the screen in mocking formation.

I had another strike; it turned out to be a four-foot needle fish that came out of the water a brilliant silver, like a bolt of lightning. It had large eyes that seemed to glare at me angrily with a mad and slightly crazed look that momentarily frightened me. Into the ice chest it went — the skipper said they were good eating.

I had chartered a half day so my time was up, but he generously gave me another hour, hoping to find drifting logs or debris that would attract dolphin fish, also known as dorado. I had caught them in Fiji and they were cooked in coconut milk — what a delicacy.

It was hard to leave the beauty of the open sea for the dirty river, but the river had its own fascination. The skipper said he was trying to form a group to help clean it up. He pointed out a restaurant that his wife owned and he invited me to breakfast the following morning.

When we arrived at the Yacht Club the soccer game was in full swing and we ordered cold beers and gave the dolphin fish to the female chef for preparation. It made a delicious lunch sauteed in butter. We had to go into town to cash travelers' checks and then we parted company with a smile and a handshake.

I spent the rest of the day lazing around reading and writing about my experiences up to that point and decided to head back to San José, call Jerry and hook up with another day or two of fishing in another area.

THE VEST
The next morning I took a taxi to the bus station. It was clear, hot and humid. I had purchased a fishing vest before leaving that had more pockets than a female kangaroo on thalidomide. The purpose was never to take it off while traveling so

that I could carry all of my valuables on my person — cash, travelers' checks, passport, driver's license (domestic and international), airplane tickets, prescription glasses, sunglasses, Gerber fishing tool, combination translator and calculator, small notebook and pens, etc. All pockets were zippered, some hidden.

I noticed people watching me fumble through the many pockets because I couldn't remember where I had stored each item. The bus had few passengers, so I took the vest off and placed it on the seat next to me, thinking it was absolutely safe and I would never, ever, forget it.

After three hot and humid hours we arrived at what is called the Coca Cola stop in San José. I staggered off the bus with a brochure in my hand with the address of my friend Tim Hodgson's hotel, the Del Rey, and showed it to the taxi driver, who could not figure out the address and kept stopping for directions.

Three quarters of an hour later I was standing at the reception desk when I was asked, as a normal procedure, for my passport. I reached for the pocket of my vest and realized I was not wearing my vest! I yelled an expletive and everyone within hearing distance turned toward me, then laughed.

Glossing the expletive over I said "stupido," realized I had left the vest on the bus. I was engulfed in sympathy when I explained, but depression was about to set in.

A taxi driver standing at the desk said "Let's go!" Driving faster than a "hijo de puta," translated means "son of a b——," we headed for the bus station. I was dazed, angry and fantasizing how generous I would be with a reward when it was handed over by a nun.

The taxi driver acted as my interpreter to the man in charge. The bus had not left to return to Puntarenas yet and they contacted the driver by radio phone. Of course there was no sign of the vest, and I went into a slump. When the taxi driver asked what was in it and I told him, he said, "Someone is going to have one hell of a party tonight."

When we returned to the hotel my first impulse was to head

for the bar and consume the first two shelves of liquor while the stuffed head of a giant blue marlin looked down on me with pity.

Instead, rallying to the cry of my ancestors, I knew it was time to pull on the old boot straps. I went to my room — knowing Tim, I had no problem securing a room without my credit card — and made nervous phone calls to Visa to cancel my credit card, American (Don't leave home without it) Express for lost traveler's checks, and the U.S. Embassy concerning my passport.

I started to calm down; everyone was so reassuring. Visa said they would Federal Express me a new card in two days, the Embassy said I could have a passport replacement in two days, and American Express said I could pick up $2,000 in travelers' checks the next day; but I had to go and fill out a police report.

I was beginning to feel euphoric. I couldn't believe my good luck followed by such bad luck.

But at the police station the language was a problem and they said I needed identification, which made me laugh. I didn't even have an interesting scar to show them.

I returned to the hotel and one of the clerks offered to return with me. Even with the help of his Spanish it was not possible to file a report until I got papers from the American Embassy. When we returned Tim spotted me and had heard the news, so we went to the bar for a consoling drink.

That night I dined at the hotel. Jerry's son Rick, who I had not seen since the Azores, turned up with his lovely Costa Rican wife, Jackie. Jerry told him I should be there and he was also a friend of Tim's.

I explained the catastrophe to Rick, who was returning to his home at Playa Carrillo on the Nicoy Peninsula on the Pacific Ocean. he was very sympathetic and said he would take me around to the embassy, American Airlines and American Express in the morning. It was going to be a four-hour drive in his father's Volkswagon van, which had been offered to me, but now that I didn't have a driver's license I couldn't drive it.

We agreed to meet in the lobby at 7 a.m. I knew I didn't

need my alarm, so I left a wakeup call that I anticipated and was in the john when the phone rang.

When I arrived in the lobby there was a lot of commotion. There was a young man on the floor with a pool of blood under his head. Two paramedics were pumping on his chest, trying to resuscitate him. A potted palm lay broken on its side, the dirt spilled over the floor. A woman onlooker was sobbing.

Outside the ambulance lights flashed and gamblers from the small lobby casino walked over and peeked nervously at the drama.

The young man had just checked out and collapsed. I found out later from Tim he had two heart attacks on the way to the hospital and died, all related to an overdose of cocaine. When his family was notified they said they didn't care, to call their attorney to make arrangements for the body to be shipped back.

It was hard to work myself into a good mood, but the errands and adventure ahead brought me back to reality.

First I got my travelers' checks without a police report or identification. I wanted to kiss both agents, but they were men — and you know how people talk.

I went to the U.S. Embassy where there were hordes of people and it looked like days of waiting, but when they found out my passport was stolen I was allowed in immediately — luckily I had travelers' checks to pay the $65 fee, and luckily they did not ask for identification, which I did not have, to cash the travelers' checks.

Everyone was cordial and efficient. After filling out forms they said a new passport would be ready the following day. I couldn't believe it.

Rick bought some avocados from a street vendor and off we rattled in the Volkswagon, which Celia had turned over in a ditch several weeks ago. The side windows wouldn't stay open, so Rick and I got the bright idea of securing them with fish hooks, string and one of my shoelaces, and over the mountains we went to Playa Carrillo.

We stopped at a roadside restaurant on the other side of the mountain. It was clean, airy and friendly, the food good but not as cheap as one would expect. A salad was around $4.00 U.S.

We took a small car ferry across the Golfo de Nicoya. It was beautiful lush countryside: orderly fields of vegetables, horses grazing in pastures, small, comfortable, well maintained fincas (farms.)

We went to Jackie's parents' home to pick up her son, but they were not in. Farther down the road a motorcycle approached us. On it were her father — a handsome man; her mother — a striking woman; and sandwiched between them, her four-year-old son from a previous marriage, so I did my arithmetic; Jackie was twenty. They were all laughing and gave me friendly smiles and passed over Jackie's son.

We stopped in Samara and I bought a bottle of rum and some Coca-Cola and limes. Rick and Jackie had rented a comfortable little home tucked away on a dirt road up in the hills. Through the thick vegetation I could see a small cove down below where Rick kept his boat.

It was getting dark and I felt like a walk. Small houses were scattered and partly hidden. I could smell baking and the aroma aroused my appetite.

Houses were lighted and I saw silhouettes, shadows, heard voices — it seemed mysterious and comforting. On the way back I became confused and felt foolish. It was dark and for quite awhile I wandered up and down dirt roads looking for Rick's house.

Jackie had prepared arroz con pollo (chicken with rice). Rick and I had a couple of rums. His passion is surfing and fishing so we talked about both and explored life ...

The next morning we drove down to the small harbor. Rick made some arrangements for cannisters of gas. He waved from shore and a friend working on one of the moored boats came in to pick him up, while I waited on the beach until Rick readied his small boat with a 90-horsepower outboard motor

It didn't take us long to get into blue water. He had two outriggers and a ship-to-shore radio. He called Jackie and then talked to some other fishermen who were catching sailfish.

Suddenly the sea became alive, the surface quivered with

roving masses of bait fish, which attracted a great variety of birds that dove, plunged and cried out.

The largest concentration of dolphin I had ever seen covorted in groups, arching their backs playfully as they leaped in unison on all sides. Hundreds of them darted under the hull like torpedoes criss-crossing inches ahead of us, showing off their acrobatic skills. I could not help but marvel, wonder and admire these graceful creatures. I wanted to be in the ocean playing with them, but I was out of their league.

My mind was free; my soul soaring. The sun, wind, waves, the birds and the fish produced a natural ablution that cleansed my soul. The sea was alive with activity and life as Rick steered the small boat among the cacaphony of sea birds and the leaping dolphins. Rick spotted yellowfin tuna. Suddenly one leaped alongside the boat, its bulbous eye momentarily defying me before it crashed back into the sea, its ridged and ragged dorsal fin cutting into the water like a saw. Rick estimated it to be over a hundred pounds.

I finally had a strike, a big heavy fish that was hard to reel in. Halfway to the boat it broke loose; we never saw it. We then hooked a small football tuna which was destined to be our dinner. We had been out over five hours and I was dehydrated from the sun and wind, slightly rocky from the constant pitch of the boat, and somewhat emotionally drained from all the excitement.

I told Rick I had had enough; my stomach was queasy and I was tired. I could see that he was disappointed and would have stayed longer at no extra cost, but I didn't want to spoil it by overdoing it.

Rick beached the boat on the sand and I jumped off the bow with the portable radio in my hand. It had been on loan and I put it in an abandoned boat on shore to be picked up by the owner.

I could hardly stand, my legs were weak and shaking. I could feel my skin burning. Puffing, I trudged through the wet sand to the shade of a palm tree.

After I caught my breath I walked up to a very inviting

restaurant overlooking the bay and ordered a salad and beer. Rick had decided not to join me. The waiter, concerned, gaped at my sunburn and I left the table and bathed my face in cool water and came up and took a long swig of cold beer. It was sharp and mildly bitter, the best beer I ever had in my life and I have had many.

I decided to return to San Jose and find another fishing adventure in spite of Rick's pleading to stay and Jackie's hospitality.

There were no flights available from the grass airstrip the next day. My only choice was the "red eye," a 3:30 a.m. bus. Jackie cooked the tuna with rice and it was delicious. I did some laundry and drank some rum. Rick paid the rent.

Rick insisted on taking me to the bus. The roosters seemed to crow all night. Rick had to turn the van around and it wouldn't go into reverse. I could hear the gears grind but nothing happened. It was a stubborn old buggy that had acted this way many times before, according to Rick. I looked at my watch and was about to head out into the dark with my heavy suitcase, which fortunately had wheels.

It kicked into gear, Rick's dog barked, I climbed in, and we were off. There was a half moon, it took all of five minutes. We were the first to arrive and we spoke in a soft breeze as the palms rustled.

People appeared out of the night and congregated in little groups, talking quietly. Rick's rent collector showed up — Rick had made a miscalculation and paid him the balance.

The light in the bus driver's house went on and soon he climbed into the bus and backed out of his yard. Rick looked at the bus and said "You didn't luck out. It's not the air conditioned one," but I didn't care and climbed aboard, thanked Rick again, and waved goodbye.

For the first twenty miles we bumped along, crossed streams and took on and discharged passengers. At least I knew I didn't have a vest to lose as I clutched the small wad of bills in my pants.

My friend Tim at the Hotel Del Rey had picked up the tab

for my hotel room on my departure to Playa Carrillo, so it was a good feeling returning to such a friendly atmosphere.

I was greeted like an old friend by the staff and given a courtyard room that was much nicer. Tim invited me to a drink at the bar to hear about my trip. As I looked around the room at the huge mounted trophy fish I was tempted to exaggerate a little, but instead I gave him the straight story, which was good enough for me.

Karen, a young English woman, was in charge of booking fishing trips. She called around to see where the action was. She mentioned "Martin," who fished for tarpon on the Rio Frio in Los Chiles on the Nicaraguan border, and that immediately appealed to me.

Karen had some difficulty contacting Martin, so I kept checking back with her. Martin had the reputation of being a good guide and a character, another Englishman. I finally spoke to Martin and we agreed on an off-season price and we arranged to pick me up the following morning for the drive north.

San José had no great appeal to me but I felt I should give it a try. A lovely desk clerk suggested a "typical" restaurant a short taxi ride away. the bellhop gave the driver the name of the restaurant and off we went. We drove and drove through crowded suburbs and if the driver spoke English he did not admit to it as I impatiently pointed to the meter. I was getting colón cancer (the local currency); he new he had a real "gringo." After several stops and "inquiries" we arrived at the restaurant — after he had shut off the meter many blocks away, a common illegal practice. He charged me 1,000 colóns, the equivalent of six and a half dollars. I knew I had been had.

It was at a small mall and I was directed to the wrong restaurant. After ordering a drink and opening the menu I saw the name and paid my bill and left. The recommended restaurant had a sign out front (the original). Competition was around the corner.

The waiters were young and friendly, the steak tough. But they exchanged it gracefully for another.

Back at the hotel they were amused by my excursion, but

upset by the taxi charge.

I decided to stroll near the hotel, which is considered safe. Prostitution is legal in Costa Rica, so the young ladies were out singly, in pairs, and in groups. Policemen carrying pistols in well-pressed khaki uniforms were prevalent and unthreatening, often talking to the prostitutes but not intimidating them. I felt secure having them in view.

On the park was a beautiful old Victorian manor called Key Largo, which reminded me of the southernmost house and my days in Key West. There was plenty of activity going in and out, and it looked safe and inviting. There was a charge of 300 colóns to get in and they stamped the back of my hand the way I did when I owned a disco in Amagansett, Long Island, so I felt at home.

The atmosphere was quite different from my place. It was crowded with young women, many very beautiful and exotic. Most wore the shortest and tightest dresses imaginable and lots of makeup. They strutted and sashayed, provocatively parading their wares.

Reasonable dinners were available and there were four crowded bars. Men sat drinking with women but there was no indecent behavior. Smiles were being constantly flashed and occasionally men would be approached and propositioned, the price always negotiable. A band was going to play later for dancing, but after a short time the amusement wore off and I thought about the next day's fishing. In the meantime men were leaving with two or three women under their arms, swaying and laughing.

The hotel had a rule. Women were allowed into your room but they had to leave their identification cards at the desk to be sure they didn't rip you off. If they came in at a late hour there was a surcharge — all very open and aboveboard.

Martin was held up by a religious parade and was pissed, not being religious himself. He was driving a red four-wheel drive diesel Toyota truck. When he got out of the cab his large frame stretched out and he offered me a wide calloused hand. He had thick curly hair, strong chiseled features and a broad grin. We hit it off immediately.

We hoisted my suitcase into the back of his truck and off we went, suddenly at the mercy of traffic moving more slowly than sugar cane molasses on a cold day. After a certain amount of cursing and taking alternate routes we were out of the crush and Martin stopped for rum and limes.

We began to get acquainted, filling in one another on each other's background. Martin was divorced and took up life as a fishing guide because he loved fishing and the outdoors and it was also a good way to earn a living.

It does not take long to get into the country and soon we were climbing into verdant hills covered with coffee bushes. At times we could see for miles down into lush valleys with streams and rivers trickling through them, each one its own Shangri-La.

We stopped at a mountaintop restaurant for lunch. The interior was made simply of native woods, the staff friendly, the food excellent and moderately priced with a mountain view.

At a hairpin turn with a mountain stream cascading below was a shrine with a large religious statue surrounded by flowers and burning candles. Cars were parked and worshippers were kneeling in prayer for the many fatalities. Martin slowed down only slightly. Martin drove fast (of which I was forewarned), but with competence, so I was at ease.

Soon we were in orange grove country that stretched for miles on the rolling hills and there was a pleasing sweet smell to the air.

We dropped down into hot, muggy country with fields of sugar cane waving gently in a moderate breeze. The towns were small and rural. Women stood with babies along the road waiting for buses.

After over four hours of driving we pulled into Los Chiles on the Nicaraguan border. It was obvious there would be no reason to stop if this had not been our destination. It was very poor and there was very little activity. It was hard to determine if we were on the main street. This was Martin's fishing base. We pulled into a motel-style facade with women and small children in front. Martin greeted them with his limited Spanish. He was well known and liked, it seemed. We checked into our room, which had the barest of essentials: two small beds, a toilet and shower. It was not the honeymoon suite but it was clean and smelled OK, in spite of a narrow gutter outside our door.

We drove down to the dock, a series of narrow cement stairs like a pyramid that ended at the river's edge. Martin's small boat and outboard were waiting for him. Two helpers shouted greetings and they came up, shook hands and carried down our gear to the boat.

The river was high and dark brown from all the recent rains as we pushed off upstream and the engine kicked over.

We came across Steve, a friend of Martin's I had met with his guide Luis at the motel. Steve was an American who married a Costa Rican and was an avid tarpon fly fisherman. Steve's guide, Luis, was a short, agile little man who was always grinning. He was Martin's sidekick. They traveled together when they had play time and scouted new fishing areas.

Our goal was tarpon on plugs — Rappalas, MirrOlures, rattletraps, etc. The air was cool from traveling at a good speed as I sat back in a comfortable swivel chair and enjoyed the scenery along the jungle river. Great flocks of white egrets rose from roosting in trees and scattered, creating a blizzard of white as we approached them. Kingfishers, their pointed beaks aiming straight ahead, flew from their perches. Cormorants with their S-curved necks fidgeted as we flew by.

We stopped and tied the boat to trees or bushes and swayed in the river's current. Martin said to be wary of wasps or killer bees, which was not a very consoling thought.

Soon tarpon began to roll and their small dorsal fin with its long last ray protruded from the water. It was exciting to see and hear these big fish in such a splendid setting. We hooked several large gar fish that feed on the surface. They were in the fifteen-pound range, a prehistoric cigar-shaped "nuisance" fish with a long, flat mouth full of needle-sharp teeth.

It began to get dark and Martin said we would return at 5 a.m. the next day. We did not have any strikes. Martin deftly planed the boat around the curves, looking for floating logs.

Back at the motel we got out the rum, Coke and limes and proceeded to philosophize and lie temperately about our mutual fishing experiences. We then went to a local restaurant where Martin had credit. It was very plain fare — rice beans and chicken — but tasty. Luis and Steve teamed up with us. Steve did not drink, but the conversation was lively, centered around fishing and women. The waitress had to stay out of Martin's reach and responded to his suggestive remarks and banter with shrieks of laughter.

We went to a local disco and joined a friend of Martin's. It was crowded and the music was so loud it was impossible to carry on a conversation. Luis and Martin danced with his friend's girlfriend. I couldn't keep my eyes open and asked Martin to take me back to the motel. It was 11 p.m. and we were going to be back on the river in a few hours.

It was totally dark outside when Luis knocked on our door. We stumbled out of bed and mumbled a good morning to each other.

Martin's helpers had the boat cleaned and gassed. One of the men had a weighted circular throw net. He adroitly flung it out and let it sink to the bottom, then drew it in. It was chock full of wiggling fish, many pan-size that would have brought a small fortune from tropical fish fanciers. It was an illegal but common practice for the fisherman to get bait and poor families to get food.

Dawn was breaking and I could smell the distinct odors of the river. People were up and about in conversation, small birds in profusion criss-crossed the river. In the boat the cool steamy morning air brushed up against my skin as I hungrily searched the shoreline for animal activity and from time to time took a sip of black coffee from the thermos.

We stopped in different areas to fish and almost always a tarpon would rise to the surface or could be heard plopping in the distance, which made it all the more frustrating because they would not hit our lures or live bait. Gar fish would attack the live bait, annoying Martin, so we would cut our line (and our losses) and move on to another location.

Martin seemed almost embarrassed that we had not hooked a tarpon, but I didn't mind. The scene was so peaceful and there were so many animals to observe. Howler monkeys came down to the water's edge on treetops, making a raucous racket. It was a disturbing sound when they screamed in unison. A large eagle sat on the top of a dead tree crying out. I did my best to imitate his call, which made him change his pitch in irritation. Next to him were two fat iguanas stretched out on limbs sunning themselves; it seemed to me reckless exposure. Cayman as large as ten feet swam within spitting range with just their eyes and snouts protruding from the water. Others basked on shore and would suddenly crash into the water after some defenseless prey.

It was around 10 a.m. and I was ravenous. Martin had mentioned a stopover on the river so I reminded him. We went further up the river; it was sultry and clammy. We came to a small wooden house on the river where laundry hung under the porch roof and several children came out and waved, their mother smiling. We tied the boat to a dead tree and scrambled up a crumbling mud bank. There were pigs and chickens in the yard and a middle-aged man with a mustache greeted us

In the distance was a large thatched hut next to a swampy lagoon. We trudged through ankle-deep mud. When we arrived at the compound, a man, his wife and young son greeted us. It was a huge empty place set up for tourists during the season called Caño Negro Lagoon Lodge. They prepared us a good breakfast of eggs, rice and beans, toast, papaya and better than usual coffee. Martin borrowed some money from me to pay the bill. Then we trudged back to the river.

Flocks of green parrots flew in a chattering mass from tree to tree. We had thrown everything at the tarpon that Martin could find in a very disorganized tackle box, so we put out live bait and hooked a machaca, a very aggressive silver-speckled fish with needlelike teeth. It performed some entertaining aerial acrobatics for us before being released.

The fish were just not cooperating. Martin had exhausted his repertoire and the relentless heat compelled us to drink frequently from the iced plastic jug of water. Martin felt it was his obligation for me to hook up with a tarpon, but the peace and activity of the river were sufficient to keep me in a tranquil mood.

We pulled anchor and went further upriver into Nicaraguan territory. Tributaries branched off in all directions. Troops of turtles soldierly scrambled off logs into the water as we approached. Brahma bulls ruminated with utter detachment along the water's edge.

For some unfathomable reason Martin chose a small stream that meandered off the river, just wide enough for our boat. There was barely enough water to draw on and the motor kept hitting objects. A mile or so later it became so shallow that Martin had to get out and push. We were up shit's creek without a paddle; Martin had left it at the dock.

I finally got out of the boat and pushed. Now and then a cayman would slide down into the water from the bank. Martin reflected aloud, "I wished I had brought my compass," which did not instill confidence. I thought a night out here would cost quite a few pints of blood — the mosquitoes were already dining on us.

In spite of our predicament I couldn't help but admire our surroundings. Birds of every description darted out of the thick vegetation of vines, orchids and bromeliades. There were more choices to take as the stream branched out. The languid current pushed us along where it was too shallow to lower the motor. Just when the stream broadened and got deeper and we were able to use the motor it quickly became shallow and we were out pushing again. We finally arrived at a deep, wide bend in the stream and Martin said the tarpon came far up into the feeder streams so we tried casting, but with no luck.

Downstream we went and the stream widened into a small river. Soon we were out into the open country of the grassland and the edge of the Caño Negro Wildlife Refuge, where we had fished earlier. I began to recognize the landmarks. Close by were storks, herons and roseate spoonbills. To my surprise I saw a red-winged blackbird, a familiar sight in Upstate New York, swaying on a reed top.

Steve was flogging the water with his fly rod, which was

just as productive as beating a dead horse. He had only one momentary hookup all day, he complained. Tarpon were rolling all around us but they snubbed all offers and it was beginning to get dark, so we packed it in.

The first rum and Coke went down like a drink in hell, as I felt my mind and body untwist from hours in the boat.

Martin offered another half day on the river; up at 4 a.m., he was a hard taskmaster.

We saw many tarpon, but again no strikes, and Martin sheepishly said it was the first time he had struck out on the river. He promised a free trip if I returned. We trolled back for snook, but all we picked up was debris on our lures.

I had a lunch of "olla de carne," literally "pot of meat," with large pieces of chayote (a green pear-shaped vegetable that grows on a vine), ayote (a pumpkin-like squash), yuca and plántano.

I said goodbye to Steve and Luis and Martin took me to Fortuna at the base of Mt. Arenal, where I had planned to fish for guapote. The three days of fishing in the jungle had worn me down.

Martin took me to a small guest house and introduced me to his friend Christopher, the owner, and it turned out he was the brother of Peter Garinsky from Guyana who was going to take me fishing on Lake Arenal. Christopher arranged to have a fishing guide pick me up at 5 a.m. the next morning. I had heard about Tabacón, where the thermal waters flow out of the Arenal volcano. My body was aching from the long hours in the boat and it was only three miles out of Fortuna.

My taxi driver spoke good English. I asked about local property and he said it was selling for around $20,000 U.S. dollars per acre.

I was not prepared for the beauty of Tabacón. All the buildings had a soft contour to them and were painted a stark white with a backdrop of rainforest vegetation. At one point I heard the rumbling of the volcano and howler monkeys. At Tabacón there are different size pools and different temperatures to soak in. The water is channeled through lava rocks surrounded by landscaped gardens of flowering plants. A waterfall of lava stone cascades steaming water onto various layers of stone where one can sit and be massaged by the force of the water. There were not many people. I had a fresh fruit punch at poolside, alternating swims and soaking, and a body massage — it was nirvana.

Since the complex had no telephones I had prearranged for the taxi driver to meet me at 6 p.m.

While I was soaking in temperate water a young blonde woman came into the pool and we struck up a conversation. It turned out she was from Argentina and spoke excellent English. While we were talking a young man, fully dressed, approached the pool and she introduced herself as Maria José and the man as Gonzalo, her brother. Gonzalo had innate Latin cordiality. He gave me a warm smile and shook my extended hand. After a brief conversation he invited me to join them for dinner with his wife, Victoria, a small pixieish woman with a shy charm.

My taxi driver arrived, so I paid him off. We settled into a delicious meal of corvina, a sea trout-like fish sauteed in butter. The conversation flowed like a river after a good rain.

Gonzalo was an architect practicing in San José. Maria José was an interior designer in Buenos Aires. Gonzalo had rented a four-wheel-drive vehicle and invited me along to see what we could of the Mt. Arenal volcano. We drove beyond the warning signs and parked in the cinders and ash. Gonzalo turned the vehicle around, pointing outward, in the event a quick getaway was required if Arenal erupted. I said I couldn't think of any nicer people to die with.

I recounted a visit to an active volcano on Tanna, part of the islands of Vanuatu in the South Pacific. Yasur volcano is very active and fearsome.

There was a light drizzle and low overhead so we could not see any volcanic activity. We sat around and joked and laughed in the darkness. I invited my friends for a nightcap in Fortuna. They were leaving the next day and I was getting up at 5 a.m. to go fishing for guapote on Lake Arenal. They went off looking for accommodations and I went to bed.

A short while later Gonzalo knocked on my door. I had left

my camera and swim trunks in his car. He gave me his address in San José and invited me to stay with them.

A few hours later my folding digital travel alarm pulsated with intermittent staccato beeps, a much too civilized and unpleasant sound. While I was brushing my teeth Christopher knocked on my door in the dark. I called out that I was alive, to make him go away.

Christopher, who has a face like Mars, pockmarked with a jagged scar that runs deep as a canyon, stared at me in the light of the street lamp and I wondered what the story was behind the scar.

We did our best to make conversation. The air was cool, the town quiet. A four-wheel-drive Toyota Land Cruiser pulled up alongside the curb towing a canvas-covered boat with an outboard.

There were two men in the cab. The one next to the driver got out and was introduced as Turcino. He climbed in the back and I sat next to the driver; neither spoke English. I was almost glad, because I felt it was too early for conversation.

Halfway to the lake I realized I had forgotten my camera and I thought, no one will believe the big fish I'm about to catch.

It was barely light when we reached Lake Arenal. There was a thick mist that clung to the lake like claws of a vulture. There was a thin, stabbing rain and I was glad to be wearing sensible clothing.

The driver backed the boat into the water and it floated off after Turcino unhitched it. I waded into the water and climbed aboard. The motor started with little effort and off we went, rain stinging my face, as I took in my surroundings of deep, dark, lush green hills. In the shallows gnarled branches of dead trees reached out like drowning arms. Lake Arenal was man-made for hydroelectric power. We had crossed the dam earlier.

The night before there was a blackout throughout most of the country and Christopher had told me with an unblinking eye it was caused by UFOs, which had often been sighted. Turcino, a handsome young dark Latin type with strong features, passed me a thermos of hot black coffee, which I welcomed.

We stopped at a graveyard of dead trees and cast with rattle-traps and deep-diving plugs. We were using open-face spinning gear with 15-pound test line. After a few casts I hooked and landed a guapote. The tackle was not in the best of condition and I couldn't believe the strength of the fish, which never came to the surface.

It made long, hard runs that made the drag whir. Each time I eased it toward the boat the fish would take off, the pole would double over, and I was sure it was going to break off. when I finally subdued it Turcino netted it. It weighed close to five pounds. Before I had seen it I was sure it was larger. My friend Peter Gorinsky had caught the record to date, slightly over eleven pounds.

We kept the fish for my dinner and I hooked several more smaller ones. Before we moved Turcino offered me a dry, mildly sweet cracker along with another gulp of black coffee.

We fished only around the submerged trees but would drift out into open water about ten feet deep. Turcino hooked into two fish that tore off nearly his whole spool of line and then broke off — they must have been monsters. I caught several more fish and kept another one as a dinner companion. The guapotes are bass-like, with thick skin and scales. They are a reddish-orange with a gray back and vertical black stripes. They have large gills, an extended dorsal fin, and fan-shaped pectoral fins.

The volcano rumbled and Turcino said, "It is saying buenos dias" (good morning). The only time I saw the volcano was during early morning fishing with Martin near the Caño Negro refuge. I could see smoke puffing out of its cone and I had photographed it.

Seventy-eight people died from an eruption in 1968. Poisonous gasses killed anyone who inhaled them, then the whole area combusted and was consumed by fire, lava flows and ash showers. The locals talk calmly, almost proudly, about the catastrophe. It is their source of pride and income.

After catching and releasing a number of small bass we decided to call it a day. It was 11 a.m.. I had hoped we would catch machacas as well, but no luck.

The driver had returned for us. A great flock of green parrots noisily flew into the nearby trees. Turcino scaled and gutted the fish. They dropped me off back in town, I tipped him, thanked him and said, "Adios, amigo."

The heat continued. I decided to wash out some of my muddied jungle fishing clothing. I had noticed in the back yard there were some clotheslines. No one was around so I knocked on the door and said "hola" (hello), and a voice answered clearly, "hola." I repeated it; so did they. When I opened the door I saw a large parrot wisely looking me over with what I thought was a bemused grin.

Later I told the story to Christopher, who had no fondness for his wife's parrots, which he was in charge of when she was away. He said he had threatened to put them in the washing machine on several occasions, which did not endear him to his wife.

That night I arranged to have my fish cooked at a nearby restaurant. I regretted my Argentine friends had left. I invited Christopher and my English-speaking taxi driver to join me.

Christopher didn't show. He said he got the time wrong and the taxi driver, Thomas, was late because of a tour guide meeting. The waiters brought out the two fish surrounded by a variety of vegetables with rice and beans that covered my table. Everyone in the restaurant gawked at me.

I ate what I could. It was beautifully prepared and everything was delicious. Finally my friend Thomas showed up with a good appetite, so we sat and talked while I watched him eat.

The next day I took the bus back to San José, a five-hour trip. The bus was clean and vendors came aboard with fresh fruit. Mothers with small children and teenagers traveling a short distance were in abundance. The mountain scenery was magnificent.

I was greeted warmly at the Hotel Del Rey. There was the possibility of staying longer if my airline ticked was not issued. That night I ate at a nearby Italian restaurant. The waiter reminded me of a Cuban waiter named Camillo who had worked for me for many years. The waiter told me he had worked at the restaurant for 43 years and he was taking his first English lessons.

They had a guitarist and singer who strolled among the tables singing romantic ballads. After dinner I asked for a cigar. It resembled aging fecal matter. When I gave the OK he took it back to the cashier, who cut it in two with scissors; why, I will never know. It tasted like the aforementioned.

The next morning I called American Airlines and they said my ticket was ready. I took a taxi and met the woman who had from the inception of the stolen ticket searched it out through their computer system. I had to pay a $50 fee to replace it.

I had a late breakfast at a typical restaurant. The dish was called gallo pinto, rice and beans fried together and served with eggs and toast.

In the afternoon I roamed around the city, a Chinese restaurant that was recommended to me never materialized. When I asked directions from a group a young man stepped forward and in English highly recommended the National Theatre across from the central park.

The park was filled with tourists and crafts people. The leather goods and ceramics were well done. A young woman made necklaces from tiny beads, some of the best work I have ever seen. There was no hustling and the craftspeople were engaging.

I was not prepared for the beauty of the National Theatre. It was built in 1890 by the coffee growers, who levied a culture tax on their exports and within seven years the theater was built. The exterior has columns and pediments, arched windows carved into the massive stone blocks, statues of dance and music grace the entrance. At the entrance is a statue of Beethoven. In the vestibule are allegorical figures of Comedy and Tragedy. The interior has great murals depicting themes of Costa Rican life and commerce. The parquet floor is made from native hardwoods. There are marble staircases and an elaborate and magnificent multitiered great hall.

In the restaurant looking out on the park, the dining room

carries out the elegance of the theater, with murals, chandeliers and high ceilings, all grand and peaceful. The staff was courteous and efficient and the food was well prepared, attractive and delicious.

I met up with Tim, the owner of the Hotel Del Rey, had a parting drink, and promised to stay in touch.

The following morning I was up at 5 a.m. to catch an 8 a.m. flight. There was already considerable activity in the streets. In one area fishmongers had barrels of fish lined up with the tails of mackerel and tuna pointing skyward like banners.

As I passed a man accidently spilled a barrel of pink shrimp into the street and was frantically trying to scrape them up.

When I settled into my seat on the plane I had time to reflect the events of the past two weeks that passed so quickly. Everything was positive and I knew it would not be long before I returned to beautiful and friendly Costa Rica.

Uruguay
(A little country with a big heart)

It is sandwiched between Brazil and Argentina like their national sandwich, the "Chivito," a delicious concoction of many things, comparable to an American Dagwood sandwich.

I had the good fortune to travel with my wife, Alison, who had just finished her third year of Spanish. She was most helpful in extricating us from many difficult situations and was often complimented on her good diction.

The most impressive aspect of the country is its people, mainly a mixture of Spanish and Italian immigrants. As a result the atmosphere is more European than Latin. They are attractive people, gracious and gifted with good humor.

Montevideo is a bustling city with a great deal of charm because of the preservation of its old European-style buildings. The Republic of Uruguay was founded in 1726 by Don Bruno Maurico de Zabara and has one of the most democratic governments in South America.

Montevideo is clean and well maintained; it is rare to see a beggar and there is a minimum of poverty apparent on the outskirts of the city. As a result crime is low and it is safe to walk anywhere, even at late hours.

The old marketplace on the port is fascinating. There is a profusion of excellent restaurants and artists and craftspeople hawking their wares.

Meat is the staple of the Uruguayan diet, mainly beef and

lamb cooked over traditional wood fires. Since nearly half of the 3 million population lives in Montevideo, it is a thriving city and taxis and buses are readily at hand. The "Rambla" is the drive and walk along the ocean. It was too cool for swimming but there were sun bathers and many fishermen angling from the rocks. It was hard to imagine the Antarctic lying frozen in the distance to the south.

Our first nights were spent at the Hotel Victoria Plaza, a bastion of grander, older times in the process of being replaced by a new structure. We were served a sumptuous buffet-style breakfast with only the highest quality of fresh fruits, juices and exceptional fruit-flavored yogurts.

Ricardo Morante, a friend from our one-time home of New Zealand, faxed me his parents' address, so we were entertained in the typical fashion, an afternoon barbecue. Most everyone has wood-burning cooking and baking ovens; it blends in so well with their native hospitality.

My friend Kirk Huffman, an anthropologist I met in Vanuatu who now lives in Ibiza in Spain, faxed me the number of his friend Analia Sandleris, a lovely woman who is a painter. She showed off Montevideo with great pride, especially the well-kept museums.

Notwithstanding the urge to spend more time in this beautiful city with its sensible pace, our time was limited, so we headed for Punta del Este on the east coast, 145 kilometers from Montevideo.

Since it was late May the resort was asleep, waiting for its rebirth during the summer in November. We chose a well-appointed and comfortable hotel at a modest rate and strolled through the not-so-small metropolis. It is a very stylish and high-tech atmosphere bordered by the sea and fine white beaches.

It was easy to imagine it in high season, with the many yachts in full sail and the bikini-clad beauties soaking up the sun. There are numerous restaurants and hotels to fit the needs of the most sophisticated and the shopping has the best of European and American goods. The summer homes reflect the enormous wealth of the part-time residents, large, stylish and manicured.

We dined at the local yacht club and strolled down to the wharf to watch the fishermen clean their catch and the sea wolves (lions) tumble with acrobatic skill as they frolicked, patiently waiting to be fed.

We wished to linger but time was not on our side, so we headed west, up the coast to Piriapolis.

The warm autumn sun bathed the city in a golden aura. Conceived in the early part of the century and inspired by European architecture, it arouses romance combined with a seaside stroll along the promenade. The Argentino hotel, which has been remodeled since it opened in 1930, has been enhanced by its preservation.

We had an extravagant and elegant lunch in a vast dining room. There were endless varieties of seafood, pates and fresh garden vegetables and desserts that would keep the doctors busy at the spa. One doctor explained the mudpacks and the marine thermal cures for rheumatism and arthritis. The attendants were in aqua-tinted uniforms and each room had complicated-looking machines with many dials, the chrome gleaming futuristically. It also has a casino.

Nearby is an ecological preserve that allows the animals to live in a natural environment. In a backdrop of hills, ponds and thick vegetation you can wander around as if you were on your own farm.

Taking leave of Piriapolis you felt you were in the Mediterranean, the white sand gleaming in the sun. People were sunning in cafes, fishermen were casting from the rocks, and a cable car transported laughing tourists up into the hills behind the hotels lacing the seashore.

We wanted to stay longer in the warm sun, but time would not allow and other adventures were waiting.

We jogged up to Ruta 9 to Cabo Polonio, not an ordinary tourist destination but highly recommended by our new Uruguayan acquaintances. We left too late and the sun was nearing the horizon as we approached the vicinity of Cabo Palonio. The area reminded me of Florida forty years ago — cattle grazing among palm trees, miles of empty shoreline, wading birds stalking their prey and festooned clumps of bushes and trees near the placid ponds.

We ran out of English-speaking natives and Alison took over with her college Spanish. We were told to go down a rutted road through fenced-off pastures to hire a jeep or a horse and wagon, the only mode of transportation capable of making the trip through the sand dunes.

Some scruffy looking but friendly men standing among lifeless buildings said there were no vehicles available and gave us some confused directions. In the meantime it had gotten dark, so we stopped at a farmhouse. A woman came to the gate with her son. He danced in the headlights of our car, playing with his shadow as it stretched across the field.

We went on to another house, but no one was home, so we drove down the highway and I spotted a car coming out of the bushes and waited for them. Alison conversed with them at length and Pedro agreed to take us to Cabo Palonio in his battered and rusted Jeep Wagoneer, which rattled and sounded more like a tractor than a car.

We followed him to his friend's house, dogs barking and sniffing at us. We transferred our luggage to the jeep, waved goodby to our new friends, and bumped and swerved through the loose sand. Alison chatted in Spanish and I patted his dog, who offered a warm nose.

We began to hear the surge and smell the sea. It was a long drive and we were tired and hungry. There is no electricity at Cabo Palonio, and lamps flickered from the occasional windows.

We pulled up at Pedro's house and were introduced to his work-weary wife, who provided us with sheets and blankets. We went to a provision store and bought a small sausage, crackers, cheese and tomatoes, and a quart of beer for me. We drove on the hard sand along the surf under a crescent moon.

Pedro pulled up alongside a small house. I could make out the outline of others in the moonlight. It had the barest of necessities: a one-burner propane stove, a sink, a toilet and a bed. We lit candles and Pedro showed us a cistern where we had to lower a bucket to get water. Then we were left on our own.

Halfway through the beer, sausage and cheese, my energy returned and I decided on a moonlight walk on the beach. Alison was too tired to join me. The lighthouse flashed, the only sign of life, and I felt very alone but peaceful.

The pounding of the surf woke me and I grabbed my camera and headed out to a mist-shrouded shore. There were make-shift homes scattered about, some showing artistic ingenuity. There was not a soul in sight as the tip of the sun burned its way upward, the air clean and salty. I took some great photographs in the pearly mist.

Alison was stirring when I returned. We had a hard time figuring out where Pedro lived. There were free-range chickens and a pig tied to a stake. A few people emerged on the land-scape, a barren but beautiful sight.

We walked to the one hotel, which was closed. Further on I saw some men in yellow oilskins, young anthropologists making a video. They were handsome and congenial and invited us to have toast and hot chocolate. One of them showed us a small black, yellow and red mottled frog named Darwin, for Charles Darwin, who had spent time researching Cabo Palonio in the 1800s. What made Darwin so unique was that he walked on all fours rather than hopped like an ordinary frog.

The young man put Darwin in a plastic bag so we could observe his undersides. He spoke with Alison in Spanish and she thought he said to release it when we were finished observing him. Later he returned for Darwin, who was somewhere in the tall grass. Alison was embarrassed and he was kind enough to say they were plentiful.

The sun had turned into a huge navel orange. We could imagine several thousand people there in the summer, but the desolation and lack of a comfortable place to stay and no restaurant spurred us on.

A young man was harnessing a pair of horses to his cart and we agreed upon a price to take us over the dunes. His wife gave me a large glass of scotch, which I spilled into the sand when no one was looking; it was a little too early for imbibing.

We decided on visiting Punta del Diablo further west, a place my Uruguayan friend Carlos Bonilla had written about in the magazine Americas put out by the Organization of American States, which had inspired this trip.

As at Cabo Palonio, the year-round inhabitants are fishermen who fish for small sharks and cure them in the sun. At the point of the peninsula are giant stones that look like backs of mammoth walruses, grey and black and worn smooth by the pounding surf so that they gleamed like highly polished leather.

There was a small restaurant at the point owned by a man who walked with the aid of a cane and who had a glass eye. He was drinking heavily due to a recent separation from his wife. His face was tomato red from years of wind, sun and drink. He was anxious for company and invited us to a drink and a plate of seaweed doughnuts.

We strolled through the empty village and a fishing boat beached itself on the incoming tide. It reminded me of a Mexican resort with the boarded-up wooden cantinas.

We decided to drive back to Montevideo and make arrangements to visit some of the ranches called "Estancias." When we returned to the Hotel Victoria Plaza, my charming friend Paula Espasandin, who acted as hostess, suggested we visit Colonia first. It was a two-and-a-half-hour drive west of Montevideo, and the oldest settlement in Uruguay. Everyone understandably speaks of it with great pride.

In the meantime we had gotten introductions and invitations to two estancias by two gracious and attractive women, Cecilia Gallinal de De Haedo of Estancia "Venado Encantado" and Clarice Buero de Santayana of Estancia "La Calera." We rented a car for a modest fee and set off at dusk along the Rambla, witnessing a spectacular sunset.

The night prevented any sightseeing and it was Saturday. Though out of season the town was lively with a group of young drummers and a horde of teenage fans parading behind them.

Our car bumped over the cobblestones and we began looking for a small hotel. The old quarter was shut down, but the shops were lighted. With Alison's Spanish we managed to find a quaint hotel on the main street.

We were tired and hungry. A fashionable restaurant beckoned, the wood fire glowed, and meats and vegetables were roasting. We shared a Chivito platter of mixed grilled meats and cheese. I had a cold draft beer called Chopp, which I remembered drinking in Brazil.

The next morning, Sunday, the town was shrouded in mist. While Alison was making herself acceptable I strolled with my camera through the old quarter. It was situated along the Rio de la Plata, a river that separates Argentina from Uruguay. Colonia was founded in 1680 by the Portuguese and later the Spanish took possession of the city; the cultural evidence of both prevailed. I viewed the Plaza Mayor (the main square), old houses with small windows and off-center doorways, an ancient drawbridge and a stone gate that secured the entrance to the once-fortified town.

Outside the city to the north is the Plaza de Toros (bullring), another reminder of the Spanish influence. The wharf was crammed with small yachts and the rigging clattered against the masts in a light breeze, sailors readying the ships for the next voyage.

I returned to our hotel to meet Alison for cafe con leche and sweet rolls. Never once on our trip did we encounter any sign of unfriendliness. The Uruguayans are most hospitable, curious and outgoing.

It is always a little sad to leave a pleasant place behind, but we were both excited about visiting the Estancias and seeing the gauchos, something I romantically identified with.

LAS ESTANCIAS

We drove north through the pampas, a flat grassland interrupted by groves of eucalyptus trees used as firewood and a cool respite for the cattle. We caught our first sight of rheas, ostrich-like flightless birds that roam the plains in groups. fortunately they are now protected — I had chased them on horseback in Brazil in the Mato Grosso.

We stopped for strong coffee and watched them prepare the wood oven for the noon meal. After several hours of driving and numerous inquiries for directions we arrived at Estancia, "Venado Encantado," a modest two-story white stucco house set back next to a stand of eucalyptus trees, a swimming pool, vegetable garden and a corral.

Cecilia came out and greeted us like an old friend, a vibrant woman with strands of kinky hair the color of straw.

She had prepared a light lunch and while I sipped a good dry Uruguayan white wine, she explained the function of the ranch.

The house was filled with trophies of her prize-winning Jersey herd and she was in the process of making a gourmet cheese which she planned to export.

Pancho, her husband, strode into the room and towered over us. His prime interest was boar hunting and he took us into his den and showed off his firearms. He showed me a clipping of a recently killed 800-pound boar.

Near the corral he had his hunting dog tied to the fence, a brute of an animal, albino-like with pink eyes, a mongrel that looked a combination of a pit bull and a mastiff. To look at him you suspected you might be a quick snack.

I always thought I was a good judge of animals, but at the port I had tried to pet a fisherman's dog who was wagging his tail. It lunged at me with a fierce snarl and I pulled my hand away just in time. I took my chance with Pancho's dog, who was whimpering and wagging his stubby tail. This time I was right and he was docile. Fortunately his short chain kept him from jumping on me, for he was a powerful animal and would have knocked me down. Pancho threw him the hind quarter of a lamb and he crunched down on it and snapped it as if it were a sparrow.

Cecilia's father's ranch was down the road, and she suggested spending the afternoon there. There had been five generations living there and it had originally comprised 200,000 hectares (roughly 2 1/2 acres per hectare). Sheep and cattle were the mainstay with limitless grazing and an abundant water supply. Her father had recently died and Cecilia was still very much affected.

We were not prepared for such beauty. It looked like an early Spanish settlement, walled in and the terra cotta tiles covered in moss. Exotic trees and flowers had been planted throughout and stately palms stood serenely over all.

It was siesta time for the gauchos and they were lounging, drinking their mate (a strong, bitter herb tea) from gourds through perforated silver spoons used as straws.

They were handsome men, healthy and rugged from ranch work. They spoke sadly when Cecilia interpreted. It was the end of an era and the ranch was being broken up. The cattle and sheep market was falling apart, now they were looking for touristas.

We went into her father's library. It smelled like my father-in-law's office (he was a collector and dealer in rare books). Cecilia's father was a learned man. She said he spoke five languages and had numerous projects educating his employees.

There was a separate building for the kitchen and dining, storehouses, a magnificent chapel in the baroque style with lavish insets of Spanish tiles. We went into the shearing shed with its antiquated machinery. Although we could not see the main house because of the sentiment attached to Cecilia's father's death, it was an imposing great house.

We returned to Cecilia's home where a barbecue was being prepared and the maids were preparing fresh dishes for our lunch.

Pancho had one of his gauchos bring one of his many favorite horses and offered me a ride. I was never a good rider and had fallen from a horse while staying on a ranch in the Mato Grosso. At age 67 I still felt fit so I mounted rather gingerly and trotted off very sedately.

The barbecue was delicious, more good wine and a slab of mutton that would have challenged Pancho's dog. With heavy heart and a full stomach we headed back to Montevideo to meetup with Luis Pardo Santayana, known as Nacho, husband of Clarice Buero, to spend four days at Estancia "La Calera".

LA CALERA

We met Nacho at his office the following day to make the trip to "La Calera." He is a handsome man, deeply tanned from many days on his ranch, lean with silvered curly hair. He gave us a broad welcoming smile and a firm handshake.

Nacho said it would be a four-hour drive in his white Mercedes sedan, accompanied by his manager, Pilar, an attractive blond. His wife, Clarice, was unable to come along. She was making preparations for a trip to Philadelphia to see her son graduate.

The weather was fair, with blue skies in our favor. Nacho became animated when he spoke of his ranch. There were six hundred wild horses, sheep and cattle of mixed breed. They had their own vegetable garden and elaborate workshops, and many gauchos and their families to maintain the ranch. We stopped along the way to buy sausage, cheese and Coca-Cola, to which Nacho and Pilar were addicted.

Considering we were all new to one another, the conversation flowed easily and there were several stops for supplies for the ranch. Throughout the stay Alison bantered flirtatiously with Nacho with her politically correct views, which Nacho for his own amusement argued against.

Nacho explained the history of La Calera. In the mid-1800s his two great-grandfathers came from Spain to make their fortunes in cattle and sheep. Nacho's plans were to turn it into a fashionable resort without losing the tradition of the ranch with the working gauchos.

Along the way Nacho stopped for a stray dog and we saw a gaucho bathing his horse in a stream. Whenever Nacho saw a gaucho on horseback with his bedroll and equipment he would say, "There is a man traveling," meaning he was on his way to another ranch, looking for work.

We encountered a man with a horse and cart that went from ranch to ranch peddling his wares, clothing and cooking utensils.

We began to see flocks of Rheas and the plains looked like the ocean at times with nothing on the horizon. At other times the landscape was dotted with horses, cattle, sheep and the ubiquitous gaucho. There were large black and white birds that ran along the ground and then took flight, crying with a kee-wee sound upon our approach.

One of the signs announcing the ranch was hanging loosely from one chain and had several bullet holes in it. Nacho had brought wire to repair it and Pilar climbed on Nacho's shoulders to insert the wire, while I held one end up.

We approached the ranch by a stony and dusty road, the pastures were bordered with stone walls. The ranch buildings were the reddish color of Georgia soil with tile roofs. We were greeted by dogs — Tuti, a small mongrel ready to give birth, and a Turkish greyhound who missed their master — gauchos and maids. It was a warm welcome.

There were many trees and flowering bushes full of birds. One felt immediately at home in such a seemingly serene setting, but on closer observance it sprang to life. A man was cutting firewood, workmen were building new guest quarters, gauchos were patiently breaking in wild horses. We were shown to our room and already a fire was burning to take the chill away from the late afternoon.

We were left on our own to explore the ranch. A small cat followed us and made us homesick for our two cats.

Steer hides were curing in the sun; we strolled into the garden where a variety of vegetables was being grown and the gardener smiled as he tended his crops. It occurred to me it would be a great place for worms if I needed bait for a fishing trip.

Bantam chickens and guinea fowl strutted among the trees and hens were laying in a box on the wall at the entrance to our room. At the approach of dusk the chickens flew up into the trees to be out of reach of wild animals.

Our first evening meal, like all others, was taken in the main building, which was filled with antique furniture and the old hunting knives Nacho collected. Each evening we sat in front of a different fireplace. There was a well-stocked bar and wine was served at all meals. The freshly baked bread and food — usually fresh lamb and beef prepared differently for lunch and dinner — were arranged attractively on large platters. Many traditional side courses were served, with the maids discreetly standing off to the side waiting for orders.

Nacho discussed his future plans for the ranch, a tennis court and a golf course. There was a beautiful swimming pool and many simple but interesting activities to keep the guests occupied.

Pilar suggested a wild mushroom hunt the following morning. We were up at 7:00 a.m. I had fresh eggs, salty bacon and freshly baked sweet rolls with hot milk and coffee. We walked up into the hills among the eucalyptus trees and found giant brown mushrooms with a mild nutty flavor which were prepared for dinner. I suggested Nacho export them to Japan. Pilar took us to a spring that was bubbling out of a rocky crevice and we all drank. That afternoon Nacho hitched a team of horses to a carriage and drove us over the plains. I felt like an early American settler crossing the prairie. We went for miles, and you could see for miles in the distilled air. We encountered many flocks of rheas and endless groups of cattle, calves and wild horses.

The next morning Nacho drove me to the area he was considering for the golf course. It already looked like a golf course, the cattle had grazed the grass so low. There were even puffball mushrooms growing that looked like golf balls.

Nacho did not forget that my passion was fishing, so he asked Pilar to take me down to a creek where I could fish. I was left alone, birds flew overhead, and wild horses came down to drink.

After several casts with a silver spoon I hooked and landed a tararira, a bronze-colored fish of about twenty inches' length and three pounds. It did not leap but made many strong runs. It had an oily blue-green head and teeth as sharp as a piranha's. I lost one and caught two more. When Pilar and Alison returned for me at lunchtime I told them I hadn't caught anything and then showed off my catch. I took them to the kitchen and fileted them and they cooked them for lunch; they were delicious.

Nacho promised a barbecue picnic and a day's fishing on a nearby river where he had a boat. I eagerly accepted.

Pilar drove the ranch van and Nacho arrived later on a motorcycle. We had brought Domingo, a gaucho, along to take me on the river. Driving over the plains we had to go through a series of paddocks that had to be opened and locked and as we passed through we bumped over the cattle grids. It was a sparkling day and a fisherman is an optimist; we were all in a jolly mood.

The fire had to be started so we gathered firewood and the grills were set up and great slabs of meat were stretched out on them. Domingo and I set out in the boat with a small outboard motor. The river was still rather high and brown. It was guarded by thick vegetation that protected many birds. I trolled, hoping to catch a famed "dorado," but had no luck. Everyone had told me November was the best time for Dorado, but I was hopeful in May.

Domingo tied up to a dead tree and we bottom fished and caught small eight-inch silvery fish and some bagre, a species of catfish about two pounds. They were mottled with leopard-like blotches of black and creamy brown skin. Their barbels were about a foot long — strange but beautiful creatures and we found out later, delicious eating.

We went back for lunch and Pilar had everything ready and Nacho had arrived. Domingo prepared his mate and we hungrily devoured an elaborate spread of food.

I was anxious to get back on the river. I had a strike casting from shore but no luck trolling, so we bottom fished for catfish and the pretty silvery fish.

We headed back to the ranch in the late afternoon, tired, full of good food and content with another beautiful day in the outdoors.

Already Nacho was arranging plans for the following day, watching the gauchos inoculate the sheep, clip the hair out of their eyes and give them a pedicure. After breakfast Pilar drove us in the van to where the sheep were being corralled. It is always dramatic to see the gauchos head out across the plains in formation, their red capes flapping in the wind and their high crowned hats silhouetted against the sky.

They gathered up several hundred sheep and forced them by yelling and waving their capes to enter the chutes, and went about their business with methodical precision.

That afternoon we leisurely walked around the ranch a little sad, knowing our visit was coming to an end. Alison wrote in her journal while I went out and photographed. We returned to our room and a crackling fire. The dogs came in with us and napped on the bed with me — what wonderful simplicity.

It was our last day at "La Calera" and I wanted to make the most of it, so I asked to be taken to a new stretch of creek to fish for the tarariras. Pilar brought a bucket of milk to feed her pet foal and then we were off.

I took in the sight of the endless plains hungrily as Pilar expertly discovered a road. She dropped me off in the early morning and said she would be back at noon.

There was a slow current and I sat in the grass looking at the sky, watching the birds fly along the water's edge and wondered about my life. Pilar, who had taught Yoga and was introspective, had mused how difficult it was to find happiness and I pondered her statement.

I finally picked up my rod and cast too energetically - I lost my lure in the bushes across the creek.

On my next cast a tararira grabbed it and ran upstream, determined to break loose. But after several minutes I brought him to shore and soon landed two others, all several pounds each. Nacho had a bonanza here and I wanted to encourage him to develop the fishing aspects of the ranch.

Working my way along the creek bank I felt the soft earth give way and I slid into the creek up to my waist and had to laugh at my own predicament as I scrambled up the bank, dripping.

Sitting in the sun with a light breeze I stretched out in the grass and dried and dozed off. Pilar arrived and laughed at my story and I photographed her in my fishing cap with my catch.

We packed, said goodbye to the maids, and hugged the dogs, then headed back to Montevideo.

We made smalltalk during the drive and I promised to send them pictures and tell all of my fishing friends of my good luck.

We arrived at sunset; the sky in the port was ablaze, a fiery red. We embraced our hosts and thanked them profusely for their warm hospitality and a memorable stay.

On our flight to Rio de Janiero I reviewed the trip in my mind and thought how fortunate we were to have shared the beauty of the purple land*. It sits quietly at the ocean's edge, waiting to be discovered.

Hosteria Estancia "La Calera"

Luis Pardo Satayana

Colonia 881P 10 Esc. 27
CP 11100 Montevideo, Uruguay
Tel. 90 48 73   FAX 92 31 77

* (In the spring the countryside is covered with a small wild purple flower, inspiring the title of a famous book, The Purple Land, by W.H. Hudson.)

Reflections

Joy Ride

I got up earlier than planned. Peering through my bedroom windows, I saw an El Greco sky, great layers of Paynes gray clouds scudding across the horizon and a slight wind making the elms shine outside my window, most of their leaves taken away by the early frost.

After a hurried croissant, coffee and the New York Times, I head for Skyline Drive and my cottage, a warm cup of coffee supported between my legs.

The news commentator spewed out disheartening news about Haiti, a country I visited as a young man in the early fifties.

I drove through the campus of Hamilton College; students crisscrossed the road like barnyard chickens and in minutes I was in the country. Holsteins were grazing on the hillside, impervious to my passing.

The sky was full of billowing clouds, imposing formations dramatically hung low over the woods. The sun lit up the remaining autumn leaves on the hillside, it was a glorious spectacle of the grand finale of autumn.

Turning onto Skyline Drive, which straddles a spine of hills, a panorama of new beauty exposed itself. The light from the east (I was traveling south) flooded the fields in a golden glow.

Brought up a Catholic, I became a fallen angel out of neglect and disbelief and at the moment felt very Unitarian. Knowing the world was full of fiends and philanthropists, I felt a great tolerance for all creeds as the heavenly light bathed the dusky cornstalks and the freshly turned chocolate earth. A stranger walking a dog on a leash alongside the road waved at me, supporting my humanitarian feelings.

I stopped at a small country post office. A friendly female clerk rejoiced in the fact it was Saturday and she had a day of rest ahead of her. I smugly boasted I was retired, and she unjealously laughed.

A wagon of bright pumpkins piled on bales of hay greeted me as I turned a bend in the road.

Soon I was bumping along on my dirt road under the pines to my camp on Leland Pond.

I gathered pine cones for my fireplace. The resin looked frosted on the cones buried among the needles of the pines, sticking to my fingers like honey. The cabin was damp, the fire started easily and fragrantly with the pine cones.

The first log I grabbed was gray and gnarled, like an elephant's leg. The flames licked at it like some hungry dragon and the smoke curled up the chimney, giving my thoughts a joy ride into the outside autumn air.

A Repast of the Past

Going back to your past may not always be easy whatever the reason, just by the mere fact it is gone, vanished, a fading footprint in the sand of time, a footnote to spent days forever gone.

It was twelve years since I sold "the farm,." I had a few chickens and ducks and a big vegetable garden from which I did my own canning. I made maple syrup, caught fish in my ponds and observed an abundance of wildlife.

My marriage was fresh and we had toddlers — a boy, Nevin, and a daughter, Josephine. This story has been told before but there is always a new slant or angle.

My friend Steve heard and read about the "farm" in one of my books so I promised to show him the place before autumn lost its luster. The day cooperated. There was a lazy warmth to the air as we headed south from my fishing camp on Leland Pond. The corn in the fields had been harvested and the roots were being plowed under, waiting for the spreading of the manure. Cabbage was being harvested, pale blue-green globes lifted on conveyor belts piled into a truck that ran along the furrows. You could smell them from the highway.

The farm stands were full of apples and root vegetables, pumpkins livened the scenery with their bright orange, remindful of Halloween due in a few days.

Everything jostled my memory as I did my best to fend off

nostalgia. It was no use; the brown fields stirred a pot of thoughts that came boiling to the surface and I skimmed off the more pleasant memories.

Each time I tried to tell Steve about the farm I seemed to be held back by some hidden hand and it became too much for me to express and I drifted off.

The robin egg blue house was still on the corner of Route 12 and Harbor Road where we turned off. How many times I had traveled that road with our small children. I can remember my son Nevin pointing at the cows in the field and saying "Moo Cow!"

Dick White, my former caretaker, had a one-man sawmill down the road to augment his meager income. He also delivered mail. We stopped by the mill where Dick, hunched over his wood splitter, didn't hear us approach.

Time had stood still. When he turned around he gave me a big grin, shut off the splitter, and gave me a bear hug. Dick's hair was as gray as the slate on Stone Quarry Road. After catching up on the family news he showed Steve his mill. The sweet smell of fresh sawdust was in the air; the giant blade looked ready for capital punishment.

Dick's parents were in nursing homes now and their house was falling apart. Dick lived in a trailer next to his parents' house. There were over twenty cats of all sizes and colors that he befriended. Oddly enough, though they lived out of doors, they were friendly and I was able to pick up several of the cute little rascals.

Judy, Dick's wife, looked the same. She is an easy-going woman with a quick smile who had me recite the news of my family.

We said goodbye and headed for Waldon Road, where my old farm is. Nothing had changed. I could see myself on the road with my tractor and trailer hauling poplar to the beavers.

Each fresh scene brought back memories. We stopped by a log cabin on a separate fifty acres I had owned. It had been vandalized and was falling apart. The beavers had moved out of the creek so it was no longer flooded.

We carried on to the main property. Everything looked the same but badly needed repair. I had three ponds and the beaver were back, which made the fourth. I had brought fishing gear so we headed down to the ponds and started casting. I had them full of fish but they had been pretty much poached out.

Some small bass followed my spinner. I caught three small, vigorous bass and a pickerel. Hardly a day went by that I didn't fish in my ponds. Steve finally caught a small bass.

There were beaver trails everywhere. The old glider swing that the owner and dear friend Lois purchased from me was sitting on a hill above the pond, so I sat and took a swing, remembering my wife Alison pregnant with Josephine.

My thoughts were jumbled as I tried to fend off the kaleidoscope of diffused memories bombarding my senses.

Dick White had mentioned the person who had renovated my cabin, Fred Stagnaro, a retired New York City police officer who was now a flight instructor at the Norwich Airport. Fred, I remembered, was a big, easy-going guy struggling to keep his family together.

We arrived at the airport and Fred's car was parked with a sign in the window. There was no one around — he was out on a flight — so I left my business card in his car window. The next day Fred called and left a message on my answering machine asking if it was the same Ralph Martell from twelve years ago. I returned his call and had an engaging conversation catching up on family histories. I promised to call him and arrange a flight with him for sightseeing purposes and to get together for old time's sake.

Several days later I arrived at my fishing camp, which is only an hour's drive from Norwich. The sky was clear except for cirrus clouds that were stretched across the sky like carded lamb's wool.

Fred answered my call and was free, so I said I would be down in slightly over an hour. After a quick warmed-over lunch that was in progress when I called, I jumped into my Explorer and headed south. It was October 29th so most of the bright colors had faded and falling leaves were blowing across the highway. I envisioned a blanket of snow that would follow in its natural course in Upstate New York.

The airport terminal was a small building cut up into small rooms not much larger than the "men's" room. The door was open; I walked in and called out Fred's name. he came out of his office, tall and rangy looking, very fit with wisps of gray wavy hair. Fred was in his late fifties. We shook hands warmly and surveyed each other for wear.

We sat and talked about old and new times. A friend of Fred's came in and paid him for the use of his plane. Fred was enthusiastic about his new profession, giving flying lessons and taking people up for sightseeing — he had overcome a fear of heights.

We went out to the tarmac where his Cessna "Warrior" was parked. It glowed attractively in the sun a metallic pale green. Fred got in first, then I climbed aboard. We started the engine and did an instrument check. Fred showed me how to use the foot pedals to control the rudder. Following a yellow line out onto the runway, I zig-zagged slightly until I got the hang of it.

We swung around into position; the wind sock hung limply. I had my own controls, which Fred encouraged me to use, and we lifted off smoothly. About the only color left was the bright golden orange of the tamaracks that would soon be losing their needles.

One of the reasons for the trip was to view my old farm from the air. I had done it once before with Alison's brother Peter, who visited with his plane.

Within minutes we were flying over it at 3,000 feet. The ponds shimmered and the 22-room farm house looked like a doll's house. The beavers had flooded the valley and there were thousands of empty acres of state land. I was thankful for having had the opportunity to live there for 10 years.

Fred explained the basics and let me bank the plane. I have been up in many small planes and have always enjoyed it, but I never felt I wanted the responsibility of being a pilot. Still, at 67 I haven't lost my sense of adventure. Last winter at Lake Placid I did both the Olympic bobsled run and the luge run, both terrifying experiences.

We spoke through our headphones, which crackled and echoed. Fred gave me some more quick instructions and pointed out the landmarks. I spotted the ponds of my friends, the Staleys, and then saw a fairly large body of water and asked Fred to swoop lower. There was not a soul on it and it was surrounded by forest. I'm always looking for a new fishing hole so I asked Fred to fly along the road that led to it. It was outside of a tiny village called East Pharsalia. Fred was good enough to backtrack a couple of times until I got my bearings.

We finished the flight without any thought on my part of becoming a pilot. Fred showed me two corporate jets from Proctor and Gamble that he would soon be taking special instructions to fly.

We parted company with a handshake and Fred waved me off in the parking lot.

Three days later, late in the morning, while at my cottage I suddenly got the urge to see the hidden lake. There was a forecast of rain but I didn't care. I put my 40-pound Kevlar canoe on top of my car, loaded my electric motor, battery and fishing gear, and drove down the highway in a youthful mood, listening to Argentine tangos.

I stopped in Norwich for lunch at the Bluebird restaurant, but being Monday, it was closed (a tradition in this part of New York state). I was directed to the Uptown restaurant by a nice lady who was the proprietor of the tobacco shop where I bought my New York Times.

The Uptown was plain as you might expect. The two waitresses were in curlers, bathrobes and fluffy slippers. It dawned on me: it was Halloween. Everyone was in a festive mood, and a witch with green lips arrived for lunch — only in America.

After consuming a glutinous concoction spread over a hot turkey sandwich and washing it down with a weak cup of coffee I bid farewell to the revelers.

It began to rain slightly but it did not dampen my spirits. I remembered what I saw from the plane and soon I was in the country on a hilly and winding road.

Several miles out of town a small sign announced "Preston" but it was invisible. Another sign indicated East Pharsalia up the road. It had a church and a body shop; the place was jumping.

Everything was as I remembered it from the air. There were scattered farms and a lot of run-down mobile homes stuck in the woods. After several turns I turned off onto a dirt road next to a trailer whose front yard was littered with trash I had seen from aloft.

A signpost with the sign missing stood forlornly at the end of a rutted road and I surmised it had been a state sign, so I took the turn through the woods. I bumped along and came out in a clearing. The lake I had seen from the air was pock marked with tiny beads of rain and mist clinging to the surface like a ghostly veil befitting of Halloween.

There was no sign of life except for bird calls in the woods. A pin cherry tree lay on its side, freshly felled by the beavers. Stumps and decayed trees stuck out of the water. There was a faint breeze, the surface rippled a dull unpolished silver. The scene was lonely but peaceful. After taking it in and filling my soul with the beauty of it, I put on my rain suit and headed out into the mist.

I trolled a large golden Phoebe. Because it was relatively shallow and there were so many submerged trees that had been flooded out by the beavers, I kept getting snagged. There were dead trees everywhere and a tiny island in the center of the lake. Everything looked mysterious in the drizzling rain. I was sure a monster fish would grab my lure. Instead the lure startled me by becoming hooked on the bottom and wouldn't come loose and it broke off.

This is the part where I am tempted to lie. The big fish that I imagined were going to strike never materialized. I brought large creek chubs that I had trapped. I stopped by the island, hooked up a minnow with a bobber, and threw it out. I then baited up a bottom fishing rig with two small minnows and sat in the rain, contented. My bobber went down halfheartedly and there were no bites on my bottom line. I picked up my lines and trolled over to several other spots and put out my lines with no luck.

The rain became more persistent but my L.L. Bean Gortex rain suit lived up to its claim and I was dry and snug except for rivulets running down my nose.

Daylight savings time was just changed and at 3 p.m. you already began to feel night closing in on you. Having brought my camera I took photographs of the desolate lake. The thought of my cheerful cabin was comforting.

I stopped at a market for potatoes for my pot roast. The checkout girl had on a rainbow wig and a clown suit which I complimented her on and left the store chuckling.

Three Brothers

A long time had passed. We were the remaining three of six brothers. Dorn, Everest and Lorne had gone their way. I'm the youngest (Ralph) at 67; Ronald is 73; and Wilfred (Willie) is on the cusp of 81.

Of a family of 17, 13 lived to maturity. Four, who I never knew, died in youth. Of the seven sisters, Della, Gertrude, Elmere, Sylvia, Gloria, and Maybelle survived. Norma, the youngest, passed away.

I was always grateful (until now) for being the youngest (Ralphie, as I was affectionately known), but watching my brothers and sister die off is very disturbing, even though it's the normal progression of life.

Thanksgiving was coming up, and there were serious problems with my marriage. My son, Nevin, at 20, is in his second year of college at Vassar, and my 17-year-old daughter, Josephine, in her last year of boarding school at Putney, Vermont, were well aware of our problems. Although very upset by the uncertainty, they were as supportive and understanding as they could be, but they were understandably hurt by it all.

They went off with my wife, Alison, to her oldest brother's home, joined by her mother and youngest brother, Paul, and their families. I decided to go to Florida to join my brothers, Ronnie and Willie.

Alison and I had been separated for several weeks. I had

been living at my cottage on Leland Pond. It was a difficult time, especially in the beginning. Fear, anger, remorse, self-pity, and loneliness attacked unmercifully from day to day.

The day before I was to leave for Florida, I picked up my friend Steven's son, Josh,– at college in Morrisville, near my cottage. I took him home, since I was going to my home in Clinton to pick up some clothing. I ran into my house apprehensively and was greeted by one of my cats, who rubbed up against me and made me feel very lonely.

Alison was not there, and I was relieved. It had been a great strain for both of us during earlier encounters. Everything seemed distant and detached, as my memory was flooded with 23 years of Thanksgivings spent together, some good and some bad.

Having traveled a great deal, I was well organized and had packed a small carry on Eddie Bauer bag that was given to me when I purchased my Ford Explorer.

It was a restless night filled with disconnected dreams, and each time I awoke I looked for signs of dawn. When my alarm went off I was in a deep sleep and didn't even want to leave my bed.

There was a feathery snow falling. I pushed the coffee switch, and soon the aroma gave me some comfort and strength. Within a short time I was leaving my cottage and punching in my alarm code.

The snow had become more intense. It was around 8 a.m , but dark because of the overcast. The snow swirled dizzily in the headlights as I squinted to see ahead. The necessary concentration kept my mind off my problems.

It snowed hard all the way to the airport, but I arrived with time to spare, and decided to park in the covered garage for fear I would have to dig myself out when I returned. Airports at holiday time are not the most uplifting place when you are alone. I began to resent all the cheerfulness and smiling faces. I kept looking back on my life, and looked forward to seeing my brothers.

The flight left Syracuse at 10:13 a.m. — on time, although the plane had to be de-iced. We stopped in Chicago, where I had to change planes, then fly on to Tampa. I wanted to call my nephew, Dorn, who worked in Chicago, but I didn't have his number.

I had given brother Willie all my flight schedules. Ronnie was due to arrive at Willie's the night before, driving in his van from Michigan. It was 4 p.m. Florida time.

No one was at the gate when I arrived, so after quite a while I called Willie, who said Ronnie had left a long time ago to come for me. I paged him. He was waiting at baggage and paged me back. We finally hooked up and took the shuttle train to the parking area. Ronnie couldn't remember where he had parked, and all I could do was look at him helplessly. It finally came back to him and we started back to Willie's. Ronnie took a different route going back, and we got lost.

Willie was slightly worried and mildly irritated. We hugged, started catching up on the news, and made a drink. Our spaghetti dinner was all prepared.

Willie is a bachelor and a fussbudget. He saves everything and has rigid routines. I always marvelled at his spartan life and good humor. He was very much a ladies' man when we shared living quarters and owned bars together in Key West in the late '40s and early '50s.

My brother Ronnie was my guardian angel when I left home at the age of 15. He had me come and live at the YMCA while he went to merchant marine school in St. Petersburg, Florida. He picked up the tab while I made a reputation of being one of the most charming and better known juvenile delinquents.

Ronnie was long divorced from a girl he met in Key West. He had two sons; one had been killed on a motorcycle. He was known affectionately as Papa Ron by his grandchildren. His grandchildren were poorly educated and developed some bad habits that translated into treating him with great disrespect, a result of their own disrupted lives. It cut into Ron deeply.

Ronnie was at heart a hippie, but it made me sad to see him at this stage of his life traveling in his van with the barest of possessions. His sight was going, and I insisted on an eye evalaution at a nearby clinic and finding a cheap trailer to live in.

Willie had a mongrel dog named Scooter, half terrier and half dachsund. He was as bright as a button and full of piss and vinegar. We became friends immediately.

Willie's place was on the water with some banana, orange and grapefruit trees. From time to time we would cast from the dock, hoping to catch a snook. Willie always has a plausible excuse for why they were not hitting.

The next day was Thanksgiving. It was clear and warm and I was thankful. We went fishing in the canals in Willie's boat, but had no luck.

Willie had a beat-up bike that I took for a ride up some back roads and went to the mall late in the afternoon. The condition of the bike did not warrant locking it. While at the mall a van pulled up beside me, silver and blue like Ronnie's. I thought it was Ronnie, but instead there were three hippie-type-looking guys, I presume in their early 30s.

They asked if I would like to have Thanksgiving dinner with them, and I graciously declined and explained my situation. They said, "God bless you," and drove away.

When I returned home, Willie was somewhat upset. He had a combination microwave and convection oven. The turkey thighs were cooking with a special dressing my father used to make with ground meat, and which I hadn't had since I was a kid. Ronnie was constantly zapping the oven into the microwave mode. Willie hadn't noticed that Ronnie hadn't turned it back to the convection oven mode, so our turkey had been electrocuted for three hours by the microwave.

It looked like something out of the Jurassic period, with little hope of even salvaging the DNA. Willie whacked it with his fist and it responded like concrete. We all managed to laugh and Willie, who never gives up, dug under the leathery carcass and found enough moist meat to make a meal. It was a tough old bird like Willie, but the day was saved.

Willie, survivor that he is, has had over two thousand radiation treatments for his skin cancer, plus innumerable operations for every imaginable kind of ailment. He laughs at it all, goes fishing by himself out in the ocean, and has boundless energy. I told him he should be in the Guinness Book of Records, and he laughed disdainfully.

Ronnie and I drank rum. Willie had his own special concoction, and the stories flowed, reviving our romantic and youthful days. After dinner we settled into a card game called bid euchre, a game all my brothers played and I grew up with in Michigan. We all bitched and Willie was constantly upbraiding us for some careless play we made and taking the time to explain our mistakes.

After pissing against the banana tree I made a few casts off the dock in the moonlight, but had no strikes.

I went to bed, happy to be with my brothers, but sad not to be with my family.

The next day started out as confusing as usual; difficult to arrive at a consensus as to how to spend the day, a normal trait with us over the years.

It was late, around 10 a.m., and we finally agreed on Hunter Lake, just a few miles up the road. Willie had lived there thirty years ago and I stayed with him in his camper. There was only one house on the lake then. It was full of nesting birds, alligators, large bass and crappies.

We stopped at a deli for sandwiches and Ronnie and Willie argued over which road to take into a large subdivision. The developers had won out. The place was full of tidy homes in a maze of winding roads. After several wrong turns that brought us back to our original destination, we gave up without catching a glimpse of the lake.

I suggested the Homosassa River up the road, which flowed into the Gulf. I had fished there with Willie thirty years ago and remembered the great quantities of bass we caught on top-water lures as eagles and ospreys soared overhead.

Citrus County is on the West Coast. It was wild and primitive then. I have a photograph hanging in my cottage of Willie and me, looking young, healthy and suntanned, with nearly a hundred sea trout (weak fish) we had caught out in the Gulf.

Things had changed. There were endless stores and developments along the highway and signs proclaiming a retirees' paradise with a modest down payment.

We found Riverside Villa, where we had stayed thirty years ago. To my dismay they didn't recognize us, or we them, and they were out of boats. They recommended a place up river. We finally found it and rented a boat and 10 hp motor. It was crowded but friendly. Brown pelicans swam alongside us as we chugged up river. We trolled, since we had to motor at idle speed to avoid injuring the manatees, which were nowhere in sight.

Willie and I thought we had strikes, so we turned around and fished the same stretch, with no luck. We tried casting for bass in the backwaters and then headed out into the Gulf. It was shallow and weedy and we caught a snake fish, a blow fish, and small bottom fish. None of the other boats was doing well, we noticed, so we headed in.

The next day I suggested visiting my old alma mater, St. Leo's Preparatory School, run by Benedictine fathers, brothers and sisters. It was in Pasco County, slightly northeast of Hudson, where Willie lived. I had not been back in fifty years.

Getting there was a shock. There were new roads, super-highways and endless developments. St. Leo's had turned into a coed, four-year college with a golf course. There were fewer than 300 students when I went there, all male. But some of the massive oaks, dripping with Spanish moss, were still there, and enough of the original buildings to stir nostalgia.

We walked down to the clear lake where I remembered many a good swim. There was little development. We walked around the grounds and went into the old chapel, where I remembered the brothers singing Gregorian chant. Next door was the stone dining hall where the sisters prepared our meals.

On our way out of the chapel a young brother in charge of the sacristy spoke to us and explained the renovations, which I felt had destroyed the old charm. He told us the theatre was going to be torn down. While at school I had a part in the production of "Charley's Aunt," so I had to see it. It didn't look like much and it was being used for storage. That took away some of my fond memories.

The next day I decided to visit a friend, John Dineen, who

lived on St. Armand's Key in Sarasota. John is a painter and has his own gallery. Willie and Ronnie decided not to go along. Willie offered the use of his car, which had exhibited some ominous intestinal rumblings on previous excursions.

The day was a Florida advertisement, all sunshine. The highways were crammed with tourists, malls and mini-marts. Endless enterprises were strung out along the highway.

It was a two-hour trip. On the causeway over to St. Armand's Key it looked like Florida as I remembered it: sparkling blue water, palm trees and white sand beaches. In the background was affluent America: shining skyscrapers and condos.

Since I arrived early I decided to treat Willie and his car to an oil change.

St. Armand's Key was bustling with well-heeled tourists. The shops were pricey and doing a brisk business. The Brubaker Gallery, John's enterprise, was upstairs over a Cuban restaurant, the Columbia. Once a landmark restaurant in Ybor City in Tampa, it was now a chain.

John was sitting at his desk, surrounded by his tropical paintings of plumed birds and colorful local scenes. According to John, our last meeting had been twenty-eight years ago, in Edgartown. Our friendship began in Key West. John suggested a lower case "g" in black on a mustard (poupon, of course) background for the supper club Willie and I owned called the Gallery Lounge. Back then Tennessee Williams came in daily for his dry vodka martinis on the rocks and brought many celebrities.

I once gave Marianne Bower permission to use an early '50s photograph I took of Tennessee, chest bared and looking very fit.

(Today, December 19, 1994, PBS ran a documentary called "Tennessee Williams: Orpheus of the American Stage." Watching Gore Vidal, whom I knew, narrate, brought back many fond memories of Key West.)

John is a month younger than me, so I eyed him anxiously to see how he was faring, while he looked me over. We quickly ticked off old acquaintances (almost all dead). I correspond with

John, who has been an honest critic of all my books and stories and who encourages me to write.

John called his wife, Lorellen, to join us at a classy and expensive restaurant nearby. She looked as healthy as a loaf of whole wheat bread. We had mutual friends from New York, so I made some inquiries.

After a cup of gazpacho and a portion of broiled red snapper, I settled into a good cup of espresso. John, gentleman that he is, insisted on picking up the tab. Comfortably full, I told John and Lorellen a slogan I invented for the Weight Watchers Club: "A waist is a terrible thing to mind." John did not laugh heartily, but it was too late — the luncheon bill was paid.

I waved goodbye under a ring of palm trees, feeling very strange about all the years that had passed by.

I missed the turnoff to the Ringling Museum I had wanted to see, and decided to keep on going. Three quarters of the way back I glanced into my rearview mirror and saw a trail of clear blue smoke. Passersby looked at me with pity. I pulled over and lifted the hood as gingerly as one would examine a stew in a dutch oven. The engine was clearly cooking. There was intense heat and smoke curled into the air around me.

A courteous highway patrolman stopped and radioed a wrecker to tow me to the nearest garage. After 45 minutes with no show, I tried the ignition and it started. I drove to the nearest exit and the car stopped dead at the intersection in the middle of the road.

It was 4 p.m. on Saturday, so I locked the car and walked to a golf driving range. The manager let me use his phone and offered to drive me back to Hudson, about 50 miles away, when he got off work at 9 p.m.

There were no garages open, so we called a friend of his down the road who had a towing service. He showed up pronto with a big flatbed and towed me home. We talked about fishing the whole way. I had called Willie to prepare him for the shock. I referred to my brother as "Willie's Rent-a-Wreck."

The next day Willie got an opinion from Ronnie and a supposedly knowledgeable neighbor. Willie had no patience and felt the car was not worth repairing, so he traded it in on the spot at the local car dealer where he had purchased it. Willie was not a man to dawdle over decisions.

(When I returned home, I called my brothers to let them know I had returned safely. Willie said to send half the cost, which I interpreted as the bill for towing , which cost him a hundred bucks. When he received my check he called and left a message on my answering machine, tersely explaining he meant half of the trade-in allowance, which was $1,500. The logic escaped me, other than the fact that I had more money than he did. Rather than create sibling animosity at this late stage in our relationship, I sent him a check.)

Willie had few modern inconveniences, as my father used to say. More to have something to do than the necessity of having clean clothes, I chose to do some laundering. Willie had a large tin tub that I filled with buckets of water from his sink tap and carried to his back yard. After adding soap I used a perforated hand plunger to agitate the clothes, then hung them on the line and rinsed them with the garden hose. I let them dry in the breeze and sun, a very rewarding experience.

All good things must come to an end, even if there isn't a beginning. Brother Ronnie volunteered to take me to the airport. Willie, an early riser, prepared our breakfast. I said goodbye with cautious sentiments.

We had ample time, according to Ronnie. On the way to the airport we talked about Ronnie's problems and touched on mine.

Ronnie became confused and made some wrong turns, uncertain of the direction we were heading. I nervously kept watching the time slip away. When Ronnie finally figured the way by watching planes flying overhead, we arrived at a tall gate that was too low for his van to pass through. We arrived at U.S. Air with only a half hour to spare, and I grabbed my bag and ran, calling out a goodbye to my brother.

Frankly Fiction

A Man of Substance

Harry Wart was a man of substance, but he abused it. He carried his name with false pride. It caused him painful ridicule and taunting from classmates and on into his later years.

Harry's resentment was seething just below the surface, so that when any humorous reference to his moniker was used, he sprung like a loaded bear trap and pummeled his assailant until the dreaded description was forever banished from his attacker's lexicon.

This distressing experience did not prevent Harry from becoming a top shoe salesman at the local bunion emporium in Biloxi. Harry, being a man with boundless energy, coupled with a manic desire for success, harbored a wealth of unrealized potential.

When Harry was not lusting after some female co-worker in the cosmetics department, his computerized brain pyramided fantasy money-making schemes that would have warranted the praise of Robert Vesco.

Handling unwashed feet and squeezing pumps onto a pampered foot where the upper extremities were more calloused than the lower gave Harry the incentive to escape the strangling clutches of the mall. Fortunately Harry had a basement at home (where all great inventions are born.)

Harry had a lackluster marriage to a woman named Mildred. Early on in the marriage the subject of children came up, but only on weekends when the grass needed cutting. Mildred could not prod Harry into keeping the grass cut at an acceptable level and would not suffer the disdain of her neighbors, so she spent her Bingo money on a riding mower.

Harry, in the bowels of his basement tinkering with some newly conceived idea, could hear the sputtering of Mildred's mower through the basement windows, and he smiled contentedly. Their cat, Amos, who was rescued from the SPCA, lay under Harry's workbench dreaming of an errant mouse. (If he didn't have to expend too much effort capturing it.)

The mower stopped and the screen door slammed. This reminded Harry he was hungry and it was lunch time. Harry climbed the broken stairs and could see the light between the steps. Mildred was pouring a glass of solar tea, wisps of hair straggled on her sweaty brow. Bits of green grass clung to her skirt as she reclined against the kitchen counter, wearily remarking, "I'm so tired I feel as though I've been ironing."

These exhausting words did not move Harry and he asked Mildred what there was for lunch — the last serious conversation of the day.

That evening, Mildred drank all the cooking sherry, opened up a can of Chung Foo chow mein, and settled into her favorite talk show, one bashing the mindless arrogance of men. This calmed her down enough to drag herself off to bed, excited about another stimulating day ahead working at the local supermarket checkout counter.

Harry was relentless in his search for perpetual motion. He knew that he had it, but how could he translate this innate kinetic inheritance into a machine to forever create energy? Like many frustrated men before him, he was baffled. His experiment fizzled like too many before. He cursed, nearly coming to tears. He heard the TV go silent and decided to wait until the sound of running water stopped in the bathroom and then dejectedly struggled up the stairs, defeated, and went to his separate bed.

Harry dreamt of futuristic machines unaided by the help of human hands, pumping away, isolated, turning wind, water and the sun into vast reservoirs of energy to be drawn upon by cluttered cities in the distance.

Abruptly he was awakened by his computerized alarm clock simulating the crow of a cock that did not exist.

Mildred had already departed for her dreary task, leaving behind limp cereal and a freckled, overripe banana for Harry to start his day.

Jill, with the overripe lips and layers of pancake makeup, came to mind, a new addition in the cosmetics department. This gave Harry the incentive to put on a fresh shirt and brush his hair before rushing out into the damp morning air.

Harry was greeted by a newly arrived shipment of shoes — boxes galore, in every style and size imaginable, enough to throw Imelda Marcos into a comatose spasm. Undaunted, he took a swig out of his newly purchased bottle of Gatoraid and went to work.

By noon he had waited on an assortment of bored housewives and methodically sorted out the newly arrived shipment, basking in the praise of the eager, promotion-minded manager.

Harry was a man capable of many tasks, and, driven by his obsessed goal, visualized a cornucopia of energy, unable to be harnessed in its profundity.

When Harry arrived home that evening there was a terse note from Mildred, weighed down by a family sized can of Campbell's chicken soup, explaining she had gone line dancing. Harry microwaved his soup and crushed several handfuls of oyster crackers into it before heading down into the basement.

Last night's experiment was running wild. Tubes were bubbling, pumps were oscillating, pendulums were swinging, cogs were grinding, expending such a terrific force that it had moved his secured workbench several feet.

Harry frantically looked for his journal of notes from the previous night. He found them, saturated in brine, undescipherable.

Energy was being expended everywhere. Harry's dream had come true. He foundered among the crazed contraption, marveling at the demonic device, and collapsed at the thought of not knowing the answer to his discovery.

When Mildred returned home, lights were on in the basement and she could hear the muffled sounds of pulsating mechanisms.

She called out to Harry, but there was no answer. Apprehensively she started down the stairs. Still wearing her cowboy boots, her heel went between the crack in the stairs, and she fell forward, knocking loose plaster from the wall, and regained her balance.

When Mildred stumbled to the foot of the stairs the noise increased and she nearly panicked. Harry, her man of substance, was covered in it. Liquid was spurting out of tubes and the whole workbench was in violent motion.

Harry was prostrate on the floor, his body convulsing.

Mildred, being the compassionate wife, realized Harry had achieved his goal but could not join in the triumph and would never know the answer to his success. With pity and tenderness she revived him, both of them saturated in the endless spewing liquid.

Harry looked at Mildred, defeated and ashamed, like a small boy who botched his first experiment with his new chemistry set.

Almost in tears, he promised to cut the grass on Saturday.

Murder at Hemlock Cove

There were two ponds called the upper and lower, deep and spring-fed. Feeder streams flowed through the marshes, bringing in baitfish, crayfish, and other delectables to feed the fat largemouth bass, chain pickerel, tiger muskies and brown trout that inhabited the mysterious depths.

The ponds were divided by a highway connected by a culvert. The lower pond was dammed to control the water level.

Even in the coldest winter the water gushed through the culvert, swirling and dimpling in tiny whirlpool patterns ,keeping the surface unfrozen for Canada geese, mallards, and some pet domestic ducks that graciously shared the space. The occasional territorial disputes caused irritating quacks and a flurry of wings as the birds beat the water.

The general scene seemed a tranquil setting. Many small cottages nestled side by side, where in the heat of the summer there were too many children, relatives and visiting friends. As with the waterfowl, clashes broke out among the residents.

A passing stranger looking objectively at the scene would have been as envious as a bachelor would feel upon witnessing marital bliss.

Like rivers with strong hidden currents, so were many of the lives at Twin Ponds. Marriages were abandoned like kittens, courtships broken off like strong fish on a light line, and lust was pursued like the many deer that populated the surrounding countryside. for the parties that were hurt, this caused an invidious mood that pervaded even the most raucous Fourth of July picnics and family reunions.

On the upper pond going south, you passed the new "Kingdom Hall," a modern church of the Jehovah's Witnesses, a proselytizing sect that annoyed potential converts in their zeal on their many rabid jaunts canvassing the area.

Backtracking past scattered farms and turning down a coarse gravel road that rattled under your car, you passed some tidy, heavily varnished log cabins that glistened, then stands of sumac and pines with a brief glimpse of the upper pond as you drove by, a quick snapshot to the eye.

You arrived at a circle with one mailbox, where the town snowplow stopped in the winter. Straight ahead was a rutted dirt road with potholes that were rarely dry. More often than not a small cottontail would dart out, undecided as to which direction to take.

At the top of the rise a lane branched off into Bert Tinkerstrom's place to the right. Straight ahead the so-called road bounced on to Ben Berkley's place and Steve Bennett's.

Ben, a dyspeptic retired auto mechanic, and Steve, a morose retired food store manager, lived side by side with a vengeance, their cottages passed down through feuding generations. Ben waited for a strong wind to come out of the west before he began to barbecue, knowing full well that Steve would bear the brunt of his barbecue sauce downwind. He would douse the grease-fed flames with water, causing billowing black clouds of smoke that made it look like a major brush fire.

Steve was fuming himself, hotter than a firecracker on the Fourth of July. He knew he had to be patient for a strong easterly wind before he could get even with Ben.

In the meantime, Bert was savoring Steve's cursing and could hear Ben and his family arguing over the amount of hamburgers and hotdogs to put on the grill.

Thus the fractious triumvirate smoldered in the haze of a midsummer nightmare. This was the tip of the unmelted iceberg. The next morning, Steve was up with his chainsaw at dawn cutting green wood. It was all for Bert's benefit, who had had a bad night's sleep from the barbecue sauce and too many beers.

Steve did not make any points with Bert, who had spent a late fruitless night arguing with his wife, Bernice, over the merits of a Bermuda cruise, which he was inclined not to take with Bernice's brother and wife (who he hated worse than his wife's honey and mustard salad dressing).

Bernice had won the argument, however, and Bert was seething over a strong cup of coffee as the noise of Steve's chainsaw bore into his brain like a dentist's drill.

The long, hot summer was just beginning, one of many to be added to the list of domestic dramas played out on the lakeshore.

Each episode became an irritant that ricocheted from one family to the other, like a pebble thrown into the water, causing concentric circles to form inward and work outward evenly.

Family arguments could not be hidden by the proximity or loss of control and temper. What was missed in volume by one party was gleefully passed on with details elaborated and invented by the other.

Property boundaries were disputed. riding mowers were sabotaged with hidden objects like land mines in the grass. Surveys were taken; stakes with red flags were driven into the ground as a legal warning of demarcation. In the dark of night they were mysteriously removed, followed by formal letters of protest from a lawyer claiming his client's property back.

Clusters of lawn chairs formed on the lawns like barricades, making sure their backs were toward their neighbors in obvious insult, but with occupants always wary some well-aimed object did not penetrate their enclave.

The assaults increased, subtle but with a territorial implication like a dog or any wild animal leaving its scent.

Motor oil was dumped in Ben's wife, Irma's, tulip bed. The next day found Steve's wife, Melissa's, laundry hung out to dry with obvious oil-stained hand prints. Fresh garbage was placed on back porches at night, shortly after marauding, possibly rabid raccoons disturbed the occupants. Petty larceny was rampant; hoes, rakes and small tools once safe had to be put under lock and key.

This once-tranquil community was locked in fear and hatred of one another. The wives, being less warlike and conciliatory, got together to form a truce. They rented Kingdom Hall, a safe haven from their battleground, to have a potluck supper and bring the feuding factions together for a cessation of hostilities.

Alcohol was prohibited on church property, but the menfolk obviously had imbibed before arriving, looking red-faced and unforgiving. The wives, sensing the recalcitrant mood, put on some dance music and each asked a different husband to dance, breaking the ice. The men loosened up and began shouting kindly remarks at one another.

When the dancers came to a halt, Bernice took advantage of the uncomfortable lull and leaped up on the stage (with a cross behind her) and gave a feisty speech admonishing the men for their lack of brotherly love.

The men, feeling the need of a strong drink, hung their heads and averted their eyes. Irma and Melissa leaped on the stage, taking advantage of the momentary repentance and preached good will toward all men. The women made the men join hands. Sobbing, they made them vow to an everlasting peace.

Kingdom Hall had never seen such rejoicing as the good-natured conversation bubbled over, while the last of Bertha's fruit salad with tiny floating marshmallows was consumed with relish and compliments.

Their hearts brimming with love and their stomachs full, they left Kingdom Hall under a full moon, laughing and back slapping. The men organized a night of drinking and fishing for bullheads aboard Steve's party boat, which had aluminum pontoons, an awning, a barbecue and a small bar.

For a while things went smoothly. There were communal pinochle games and horseshoe tournaments, but there were some bad losers. Bert and Ben nearly came to blows over a call in Ben's favor at horseshoes. During a heated game of pinochle Steve threw his cards in the air, accusing Bert of cheating. Bert, his honor in question, doused Steve with the remainder of his beer.

Shortly after these fractious incidents the rather nasty pranks became evident again. Bert's prize vegetable garden was dug up, followed by a potato stuck into Steve's exhaust pipe on his car, nearly asphyxiating him. Ben's close call at horseshoes did not go unnoticed and he found his gas tank siphoned off one morning when he was due to leave for his weekly binge at Off-Track Betting.

The wives were exasperated. They joined forces in retaliation and organized a gambling jaunt to Turning Stone, a newly opened casino run by the enterprising Oneida Indians. The men reluctantly agreed to go.

Searchlights played in the air to attract attention for miles around, reflecting off the low clouds. As you approached it looked like UFOS. It was a rather garish place with chrome and glass gleaming everywhere. In the entrance, a large fake stone turned slowly on its base like a chicken roasting on the rotisserie of the Jolly Butcher market.

The main room was gargantuan. Glass chandeliers illuminated a room bustling with dealers and waitresses in prim costumes. Steve was disappointed; he expected something closer to Frederick's of Hollywood or Victoria's Secret.

It could have been named Kingdom Hall; no alcohol was served. Bert treated the ladies to a round of capuccinos at a block-long bar that displayed a variety of soft drinks. The capuccino was weak, topped with a dollop of imitation whipped cream; no one seemed to care.

The women branched off from the men and headed for the Bingo section, where a large lighted board flashed the numbers that were called out, looking like the scoreboard at yankee Stadium.

Ben and Steve sat at a roulette-style game where the minimum bet was a dollar. They each cashed twenty dollar bills. In no time at all Steve lost ten dollars and was annoyed because Ben was winning. A fat lady next to Steve with a cigarette dangling out of her mouth silently spread five dollar chips on a series of numbers, looking disdainfully at Ben and Steve and their dollar bets.

The craps tables were full, the large red plastic dice were hurled against the curved railing, tumbling on the green felt accompanied by watchful eyes and gasps. Some mild cursing was stifled.

Bert was nowhere in sight. Ben and Steve headed for the five dollar Blackjack tables. They sat down and cashed another twenty. A waitress with a plastic smile offered them sodas and each took a Coke. The dealer was a young black woman who was very facile. She deftly shuffled large stacks of cards and had the players cut them. She wasted no time in winning their money. Steve got nervous and knocked over his Coke onto the playing field, annoying everyone. Ben had one chip left and lost. They got up, both relieved of their hard-earned bucks, although it did little to cement their friendship.

The women were laughing, happy with one another, the evening and their winnings. They drove home in Bert's car, the women talking animatedly, the men sullen.

Life heated up on the pond, accompanied by August's heat. Tempers flared like the flames of the barbecue. The sermons at Kingdom Hall were forgotten and the losses at the casino remembered. Devilish pranks resumed, arousing the ire of the frustrated wives. They gave an ultimatum to their husbands which went unheard - live in peace or suffer the consequences.

In spite of their differences, Ben, Bert and Steve agreed to keep the night bullhead fishing date. A chest of ice-cold beer was a requisite, as well as a bottle of 110-proof bourbon. It was now early September and there was a definite chill in the air, encouraging many preliminary swigs from the bottle to fend off the night air and bring warmth to a friendship that didn't exist.

They assembled their short rods and for bait used fat garden worms that had been dug up and stored weeks ahead of time.

They set out from Steve's dock in the pitch black of night with kerosene lanterns glowing from the bow and stern. They had consumed enough bourbon to be in high spirits and friendly toward one another, sentimentally referring to happier bygone days.

Irma, Bernice and Melissa had made plans weeks ahead of time. They had given up on their husbands' behavior long ago and had concentrated on increasing their life insurance. It was mutually agreed they should all benefit from their plans, sworn to secrecy with the thought of living in everlasting peace.

The wives arrived on the dock laughing at their already half-drunk husbands and kissed them, which was to be a final farewell. Steve was at the helm proudly in command, the 25-horsepower Mercury outboard pushing the light craft gently through the chop, the waves making a hollow sound against the pontoons. They agreed to fish around the pilings that once supported the old ice house when ice was cut from the lake and pulled by teams of horses and stored in straw for summer's use.

Bert cautioned Steve about the jagged, rusted nails that stuck out from the rotted pilings. Steve, taking a long swig from the bourbon bottle, laughed, assuring Bert he was in full command. Ben squinted in the darkness, a cold beer clenched in his hand, seeing Steve's face glow in the lantern light. A cement block lowered on a clothesline was lowered as an anchor.

In the meantime, their wives got into the van and drove with the lights off to the other side of the pond, where their husbands would be fishing.

Bernice, it was decided, would be the hit lady. She had taken Bert's .22-caliber rifle. It was quiet, had a good range, and make a small hole.

They parked off the road behind a clump of high bushes, well out of sight. They all wore dark clothing and not a word was said. But all were very determined.

They walked through dried stands of cornstalks that made a faint rustle, but in the open field their feet tangled in pumpkin and squash vines. They stumbled on the large vegetables in the fields. Steadying themselves, they crept silently down to the water's edge. They could hear their husbands laughing and making some disparaging remarks regarding them, giving Bernice an itchy finger.

In the glow of the lantern they saw Bert haul in a black shiny bullhead, boasting it was his eleventh.

With Irma and Melissa at her side squeezing her for comfort and assurance, Bernice aimed the rifle below the light of the lantern. A sharp crack followed by two more that echoed across the water. The men shouted, laughing, reaching for the bourbon.

Within minutes the boat listed and the pontoons gurgled as they filled with water. The men panicked and all rushed to one side; the boat capsized, dumping all three flailing into the water, cursing and screaming.

It was a well-known fact that none of the men had ever learned to swim, something they very much regretted on this night. The water was cold and deep. Bert and Steve clung to one another and pulled themselves under. Ben tried clinging to the pilings, but the rusty nails cut into his hands. Bleeding, he let go and sank, joining the bullheads.

The wives, waiting to hear the final outcome to be sure there were no survivors, ran back through the field to their car and drove home, shivering.

Someone on shore heard the commotion and called the police. They brought a small boat with a searchlight and discovered Steve's boat with one pontoon jutting out of the water near the pilings, but no sign of any survivors. They went back to shore and called for divers and scuba gear. Well into the night the bodies were recovered and identified, and each wife was notified.

They all perfected uncontrolled grief and were comforted by the police and their neighbors. They were given sedatives and told an autopsy would be performed in the morning.

It was determined that each man had a disproportionate amount of alcohol in his system and it was surmised that a sudden burst of uncontrolled high speed had taken them into the pilings. The protruding nails tore holes in the pontoons and it quickly sank the boat.

The twin pond association held a benefit for the wives and families. There was an overflowing memorial service at Kingdom Hall.

After the proper amount of mourning and consolation, the insurance monies were paid off and Bernice, Irma and Melissa were frequently seen at the Turning Stone Casino, this time able to afford the Blackjack tables and occasional cruises to Bermuda.

The Infirmary

It was a beautiful summer day, yellow cabbage butterflies danced in the air, elusive and frolicsome. Out of the clear, bright blue sky the sun blazed brilliant, giving the earth a special radiance.

Harriet "Bunny" Reynolds looked out of her room through faded gauze curtains, down on a peaceful scene of cows grazing. A faded red barn glowed warmly in the sun. Willard, one of the hired hands, stood in the doorway of the barn with a gleaming stainless steel pail of milk. Somewhere in the dark hollow tunnel of her memory she heard her mother call out, "Harriet, you did a poor job of weeding the radishes," and she winced when she remembered the looks of disapproval on her mother's face.

Harriet was wearing a worn terrycloth green bathrobe with numerous food stains. She was used to better things and she felt ashamed when she looked in the mirror. None of the useless objects around her were familiar: a small bureau with peeling paint; a straightback chair with a vinyl seat cushion; the slightly distorted small mirror hanging over the bureau added to the unreality. There were several paperbacks on a bedside table, some with the covers torn and pages missing. A small closet was empty except for an assortment of left-behind clothes hangers reminding her of a vacant house she once played in as a child.

Harriet thought, "I could do a better job on that radish bed," and she went to the door. Her thin bony arm showed the veins, her nails were yellowed and cracked as she twisted the white porcelain knob. The door was locked.

Bunny began to cry. The tears felt warm and tasted salty, which gave her some comfort. She felt she had disappointed her mother again and she felt guilty. Maybe she would let her hoe the potatoes next time; that was less exacting.

Bunny stared at the wallpaper with the small flowered print. It went in and out of focus. She heard the crunch of gravel outside and she went to the window.

A small gray car stopped at the entrance. An older gentleman got out and opened the back door and reached in, taking the hand of a woman whose white hair seemed to glow when she stepped out, with some effort, into the sunshine.

Harold the hunchback, who had a freshly shaven head, appeared dramatically, still wearing his rubber gloves from working in the kitchen. He assisted the aged woman and took a shopping bag containing her belongings.

All three disappeared under the portico. The car's motor was still running; obviously the driver had intended a hasty departure.

Bunny went back to the bed, sat down and stared at the tattered rag rug under her feet.

After a long time examining her grimy sneakers she got up and went over to the mirror above the bureau and looked at her sunken image. For a moment she thought it was a trick — was that her mother staring back? She moved out of range of her reflection and stepped back again into view. Another image appeared, startling her, and she was puzzled how she could have become so old overnight.

There was a knock on the door and she heard a key inserted. She froze like a rabbit in headlights, feeling apprehensive.

The door opened and Albert — another attendant, with flaming red hair — announced in a quiet, unthreatening voice it was time for lunch.

Albert's white jacket was soiled and his eyes shifted away

from Bunny to the window, making sure the padlock on the iron bars was in place.

Albert took Bunny's hand as if they were going to waltz, and led her out of the room and down a narrow hallway with many doors, to a small elevator. Bunny went in ahead. Albert closed the door and stretched the accordian-like lattice steel frame across the threshold, it snapped into place.

They magically and slowly descended. It was only three floors, but it seemed like an eternity for Bunny, who could smell Albert's unpleasant body odors. The little glass window on the main floor's door matched up with the elevator and Albert pushed it open into the foyer.

There seemed to be considerable activity due to the new arrival. She saw the newly arrived gentleman writing a check at the desk and talking to Martha, the proprietor. He seemed agitated, but Martha was calm as she accepted the check and gave him a reassuring professional smile. They exchanged some whispered conversation and the man turned and headed for the exit, giving Bunny a helpless and desperate grimace.

Albert, squeezing Bunny's hand, led her into the dining room. There were several occupied tables of elderly guests of mixed gender. They all seemed vaguely familiar, but no one offered any recognition, so Albert took her over to a small table near a window overlooking the back lawn and barn.

There was a small sink with purple flowers in a vase. Bunny knew her mother expected her to wash her hands before eating, so she went over to the sink and ran water that was ice cold. She quickly drew away and wiped her hands on her dress. She bent over to smell the flowers, only to be greeted by a plastic fragrance — they were artificial.

Charlie, the young waiter who looked like a wrestler, came to take her order. He wore a tee-shirt with a humorous message and a baseball cap on backwards. After studying the menu Bunny ordered a tuna fish sandwich and iced tea.

Bunny sat calmly staring out the window. A tractor drove by pulling a wagon full of hay and she could hear a chainsaw in the distance. Above the coffee machine was a hand-printed sign that said NO PROFANITY.

Charlie returned with her sandwich. On the side was a crisp wrinkled pickle and potato chips. A few minutes later he returned with the iced tea. Bunny noticed there was no lemon and requested it. Charlie looked at her as if she had ordered caviar; he said nothing and walked away.

When Bunny finished her sandwich she noticed Albert lurking near the kitchen, impatiently waiting to take her back to her room. Bunny daintily patted her lips with the paper napkin and thought how nice it would be to take a walk in the sunshine as she stared out the window — she might even be willing to work in the garden.

The newcomer was brought into the dining room looking bewildered. She was passed over to Albert to dispense with. For a second Albert's face almost looked intelligent, his eyes brightening as he led his new ward over to Bunny's table and introduced her to Peggy Mitchell.

Peggy was nervous and ungainly, but Bunny's comforting, childish smile put her at ease.

Neither one had anything to say; they couldn't remember their pasts. Although Bunny's stomach felt queasy she said the food was good and recommended the tuna fish sandwich.

They sat mostly in silence, two lost souls returned to the innocence of their youth. Bunny had a vague recollection of being dropped off for lunch by someone familiar.

Without asking, Charlie placed a small dish of vanilla ice cream and a cookie in front of them. They thanked him and smiled at one another in unison.

When they finished under Albert's watchful eye, he came over for them. He made a triangle out of each arm and they threaded their frail hands through his arms as if they were going off to a cotillion.

On the way past the coffee machine, Albert turned to Bunny and asked her to explain the meaning of the sign.

The High Price of Art

Bruno Marcavici stood, meditatively clutching a fistful of brushes like a young man about to offer a bouquet of flowers to his beloved. The sun slanted through the skylight, particles of dust dancing in the beam like some micro-galaxy.

His palette drooped in his listless left hand. Bright gobs of paint swirled and intermingled in confusion, like some surreal technicolor planetary landscape.

Bruno's grey-flecked beard complemented his palette. After applying a few deft and brooding strokes to his canvas he would stroke his beard in contemplation, transferring the "bouquet garni" of oils from his palette and brushes to his beard, giving him a carnival look.

Bruno's girth belied his dexterity. Although his formidable paunch protruded into his work, also taking on a menu of colors, he danced excitedly when he felt he executed the right piece to the emerging puzzle, and he pranced and twirled like a trained circus bear.

The large canvas was held firmly in place by a large makeshift scaffolding. The brunt of Bruno's weight was supported by a flimsy narrow plank that bowed under his bulging, darting movements. Bruno moved parallel to his canvas, much like a locomotive full of steam, nearly running off the tracks in his excitement.

Down below was his subject reclining on black velvet, the

soft curves of her milky skin contrasted by her flowing raven hair, which glistened in the sunlight. Olga was more than a model; she was Bruno's all-consuming passion. She was his instrument of love, which he was in the process of depicting abstractly. The subject, a classical guitar, molded into the sensuous curves of Olga's body and becoming one.

They had made love earlier and the whole process of desire was welling up inside him again as he gazed down on Olga's sunlit-warmed, glowing flesh. Bruno thought sex and good straight malt whiskey were things one could not overindulge in.

At that moment Olga shifted her body. Her skin creased and rippled, catching the early morning sun in each crevice. She turned her face upward with a devilish and angelic expression. The high cheekbones and Mayan nose cast angular shadows, accenting her large almond-shaped eyes and reflecting her ancient history. Olga was totally secure in her beauty, coupled with her mystical heritage.

Bruno's attention abruptly shifted from the canvas to the flesh. Aroused, he returned Olga's enigmatic, penetrating stare. Helpless, he foundered on the narrow plank, nearly losing his balance, mesmerized by his impending lust.

Bruno spasmodically dropped his palette and brushes, the scaffolding wavering perilously under the weight of his trembling hulk. He slithered through the fresh paint droppings that spattered the walkway under his painting, groping wildly for a foothold as he inched his way to the ladder.

His painter's smock became entangled on the projecting side rail of the ladder as he began to descend. He ripped it free, cursing, as perspiration ran from his forehead into the concoction of paint in his beard, creating a rainbow of colors and giving him a mad and hysterical look.

Olga was unperturbed by all of this, having on many occasions experienced this wild hold she had on Bruno and the depraved behavior that possessed him when his passion ran amok.

Bruno, racing toward the platform where Olga languished, tore off his clothes at each feverish step. Olga waited pliantly, unmoved by her lover's hunger.

Bruno flung himself upon her, out of control, and plucked and strummed Olga's body, sedulous in his goal: imagining he was Andrés Segovia, performing Bach.

(A mid-life fantasy)

The Bassoon
(Sequel to The Piano)

Theonia Swineheart was a dour woman who resented parting with her picayune dowry when she became betrothed to Bruno Weingart. It was not a match made in heaven, but arranged by her father, a long-winded politician whose endurance and lungs Theonia inherited. This induced her to choose the bassoon, which appealed to her baser instincts.

The sonorous, growling tone of the bassoon imbedded in her a frightening aspect, like distant thunder signaling the approach of a severe storm.

Playing the instrument was like making love to a swan. Its long curved stem brought to the lips aroused carnal sensations and the double reed fluttered within the soft flesh of her mouth, arousing a craving for a much-needed lover. As the intensity of her playing increased, tendrils of hair broke loose from her tight bun and clung to the sweat of her brow. Theonia's eyes glazed over like a Victorian doll as she played in a trance-like state.

Bruno, her father's guest, first heard her perform in their drawing room. The candles flickered shadows across Theonia's face, accenting the sunken cheeks and her dilated eyes, which appeared narcotic.

The musicians were performing a fugue, with harpsichord, harp and bassoon. They conversed instrumentally, imitating each phrase and developing contrapuntally, all notes absorbed by the hushed audience and heavy drapes and carpeting, the fugacious notes fell like petals of a late blooming rose. Inwardly Bruno reacted like a Weimaraner straining at his leash with the fresh scent of a stag in his nostrils.

When Theonia emerged from her trance at the end of the concert, Bruno approached her with her father and there was a formal introduction. Bruno was tall and wide-framed, his face covered with a thick chestnut beard. Glints of rust caught the candlelight and sparkled when his face became animated. It reminded Theonia of her roan foal, and she had to suppress an urge to stroke it.

Theonia's reticence was overcome by Bruno's boldness, his nostrils flared like a mastiff in heat and he extended a powerful calloused hand, the product of a shipwright. The grasp was firm but gentle, a gentle squeeze that conveyed to Theonia that the meeting was an omen. Her father looked on approvingly, having great hopes he would soon be unburdened by matrimony.

Mr. Swineheart also had a younger daughter, Orgaverga, who played the organ. She also had a sour, withdrawn disposition that repelled many a young politician, who Mr. Swineheart brought home in the hope of retiring to a more solitary and sane life, which he so desperately craved after the loss of his wife from consumption.

Bruno extended an invitation to tea the following afternoon. Theonia austerely and dutifully accepted under the scrutiny of her father.

The next day being Sunday, Bruno had respite from the shipyard and arranged to meet Theonia after an early morning church service to which Mr. Swineheart donated beyond his customary generosity in the hope a higher being would intercede for a quick marriage.

Promptly at 11 a.m., Bruno arrived in a hired carriage and whisked Theonia off to a reputable tea shop. Theonia reflected her sombre mood in her dress, a mixture of grays, black and starched whites exhibiting her hidden tendency for the nunnery. The clip-clop of the horses' hooves broke the silence as they nervously attempted conversation over the fine spring weather that was most welcome after a harsh winter.

The tea shop was prim and proper. They dined on sweet biscuits and a fragrant floral tea. Bruno was patient and receptive. Theonia surprised herself by conveying with great passion her love of music and her inseparable marriage to the bassoon.

Bruno sensed something repressed and exciting, which prompted his own confession for the love of the sea and a desire to roam the vast oceans with a suitable companion who shared his sense of adventure.

For the first time in Theonia's stifled life, something stirred in her bosom (other than the bassoon). Bruno both frightened and excited her, and she realized this could be a timely escape from her tyrannical father and her jealous sister.

The meetings between Bruno and Theonia became more frequent, which Theonia's father observed avariciously in the hope Theonia would soon be on the high seas. During their courtship Theonia exposed Bruno to the culture of classical music.

On an afternoon when the house was empty of her father and sister, Theonia gave a solo concert for Bruno. When Bruno, who had so often been captivated by Theonia's double tonguing of her bassoon, found himself alone with her, he could not control himself and fell upon her during a tremulous passage. Theonia fell backward, getting caught in the heavy damask drapes, as Bruno after hours of concentration imitated Theonia's double tonguing and aroused in her passions she did not know existed. She knew a confined trip with Bruno devouring her on the crest of a wave would be the height of passion rewarded.

They quickly agreed to marriage and a long voyage. Theonia's father was jubilant and her sister happy to have all of her father's attention. Bruno built his dream boat, and a simple wedding ceremony was held. A small gathering of well-wishers gathered at the wharf to see them off. Orgaverga and her father found it hard to conceal the joy they felt at not having to ever again listen to the interminable scale of the bassoon.

They were insouciant as they waved goodby, Bruno staunchly at the helm in a light breeze, buoys clanging, gulls crying, Theonia dabbing at her eyes with a delicate embroidered handkerchief as she waved and they slowly merged with the horizon.

Bruno had chosen HIVA-OA, a small island in the Marquesas in the South Pacific, as their destination. He had seen photographs of the beautiful women of the island and they were noted for their lack of sexual inhibition.

The first part of the voyage was calm and Theonia would play the bassoon under a canopy of stars. Then came the rage of King Neptune, and the fury of the storm kept them down below for fear of being washed overboard. When they were able to eat, what was left of their rations was potatoes and cabbage to avoid getting scurvy. Their fresh water finished, they relied on rain storms to catch fresh water in cooking pots.

The dream of romantic nights and unbridled passion vanished with the good weather. Pale and desperate, they looked at one another through sunken eyes and after many weeks with Theonia clutching her bassoon like an only child, they sighted land.

From the dark blue of the Atlantic Ocean and frigid weather, the jade green sea of the Pacific appeared, accompanied by languid breezes. In the distance verdant mountains shrouded in mist poked their peaks up into billowing cloud formations.

Bruno, haggard but in command, guided his ship between a necklace of coral into a calm lagoon. Theonia had become mute from her sea sickness and many days below deck.

The coconut palm-fringed shore came into focus and thatch-roofed houses could be seen among the palms. There were flowers everywhere and brilliant birds and birdsong filled the air. Dolphins cavorted alongside the bow of the ship and several outrigger canoes pushed off from shore laden with natives and fruit.

The natives' laughter carried over the water, and some jumped off the canoes and swam alongside the ship. The men were short, thick-bodied and muscular from pearl diving, fishing and gardening. They had matted black hair and some wore a small mustache. Theonia's senses revived and she made grunts of approval.

The women had flowers in their hair; their bodies and hair

glowed from coconut oil. They had small, well-formed breasts and they laughed constantly, displaying even white teeth accented by their smooth tawny skin.

Drums beat on shore, ropes were lowered and both men and women came aboard carrying garlands of fresh fragrant flowers, which they draped over Bruno's and Theonia's necks. Baskets were lowered and filled with a variety of exotic fruits. Both Bruno and Theonia were captivated by the beauty and uninhibited sensuality of their hosts after living in such a repressive society.

Bruno dropped anchor near shore and they were taken by outrigger to the village. Already a welcome feast was being prepared and the terrified squealing of the pigs being butchered in the bush heightened the excitement. Pits were dug and fires started. A mild alcoholic drink made from fermented coconut milk was passed around and the dancing started. The bodies swayed and gyrated like snakes, seemingly without a bone. It was like the garden of Eden before the apple was eaten.

Theonia clutched her prize possession, the bassoon, which aroused everyone's curiosity. The swaying bodies, the laughter, the mild drink and the beauty of the setting infused in her a sensuality she never knew existed. She put the bassoon to her lips and began to play, the drummers softened their beat, and a haunting melody wafted out to sea and up into the mountains.

Suddenly Theonia was a white goddess. Both men and women gathered around her and touched her and the bassoon, as if they both were sacred objects and she was immediately elevated to a deity in their eyes.

Bruno was not unnoticed with his fair skin and chestnut beard. Young, unbashful maidens sat at his feet and stroked his beard.

Makuto, a handsome young warrior, massaged Theonia's feet as she played, which inspired her to reach notes she never would have attempted in the drawing room.

They were offered a modest hut and a maid after the night's festivities. Makuto was hopelessly in love with the goddess and followed them to their hut, falling asleep in the sand near the entrance.

Bruno and Theonia adapted quickly into the customs of the village. They ate sea centipedes, spear fished, dove for pearls, went on wild boar hunts, learned to make tapa cloth, and dined on strange fish and sea turtles.

When Bruno went off on a hunting or fishing expedition, Theonia played her bassoon in a grotto near an emerald pool deep in the jungle. Makuto followed her and gathered flowers and wild fruit for her. He massaged her feet with sweet smelling coconut oil and slowly he traveled up Theonia's body into each crevice with his oily fingers, until Theonia gasped; the notes from her bassoon became further apart and she lost control of her breathing as Makuto's tongue and fingers turned Theonia into the instrument of his love and her body sang and vibrated with passion as waves of ecstasy throbbed through her body like the tide at full moon.

Bruno, returning from a wild boar hunt that sometimes lasted for several days, noticed Theonia taking on a soft beauty and she began to form words and became animated at the stirring of a leaf in a breeze. But his attention toward her was repulsed and although he had flirtations with several local beauties, he was jealous of Theonia and angered by her rejection.

Pretending to go off on another hunting trip, he followed Theonia to the grotto. Soon Makuto arrived after Theonia began to play her bassoon, and the ritual lovemaking with Makuto slithering over her, their well greased bodies in harmony, undulating, both moaning with uncontrolled passion as their stroking and thrusting reached a crescendo and they fell exhausted into one another's arms.

Bruno, like a lion crouched in the foliage, was both aroused and enraged by what he had witnessed. He crept silently away, defeated, plotting some horrible fate for the lovers.

Bruno's first act of recrimination was to stuff an overripe breadfruit that was fermenting, sour and foul-smelling into the opening of Theonia's bassoon, making it impossible for her to beguile her lover with her playing.

Theonia was not dismayed during the cleansing period of

her bassoon. Having recovered her voice, she wooed her lover with ballads of undying love.

Bruno, observing that encounters of rage and accusations were having no effect on the lovers, consulted with the village chief and medicine man. In the past, many of the natives were eaters of men, usually the flesh of an opposing warrior that they ate for vengeance's sake. Since this was a battle for love, the medicine man suggested that Bruno kill and eat his wife's lover. Bruno gave the medicine man a few coins for his consultation and promptly went into the bush and vomited.

Theonia had never been happier, although the temporary loss of her bassoon was like having an unwanted abortion. Makuto was an ardent lover who knew no restraint. Theonia's puritanical body and mind opened up to Makuto like the night-blooming jasmine. Whenever she experienced physical and mental ecstasy she felt was beyond her capacity to endure, she climbed to a higher plateau like the snow-covered peaks in the distance, each excursion of love a near religious experience increasing the elevation.

Bruno's fury raged beneath a seemingly tranquil exterior, like the sacred volcanos of Mt. Uomoa that rumbled forebodingly, striking fear into the would-be sinners.

Bruno in his distraction disregarded all personal grooming. His hair became long and wild, his beard completely engulfed his face so that his eyes burned like embers beneath his flaming beard. His thick eyebrows jutted out like wisps of smoke from a smoldering fire. He was heard babbling at all hours of the night, a pitiful man at the mercy of his waking nightmares.

Time was measured from dawn to dusk and the growling of the stomach that called for food. Bruno's melancholy took away his appetite, so that he rapidly lost weight and began to look like a hairy tarantula.

Delirious with a full moon filtering through the palms and shimmering over the lagoon, Bruno lay slobbering in his bed of tears, the night doves' cooing overhead, rapturous with their mates, adding to his discomfort. Far in the distance, from the grotto came the deep wailing cry of Theonia's bassoon, interspersed with her shrill throbbing voice serenading Makuto.

In a crazed frenzy Bruno leaped from his bed of banana leaves, grabbed his boar hunting spear, and crashed into the jungle in the direction of the tormenting sounds.

The path was slippery from an early evening rain, and animals scurried away underfoot. His foot caught in a vine and he fell to the ground cursing. Bruno's mind went back to the drawing room where he first met Theonia and he felt he was in a dream.

Suddenly the ground gave under him and he fell a long distance into a fermenting mush of breadfruit that had been stored in a deep pit for a religious festival soon to take place.

Bruno was too weak to even call out. He lay in the stench of the sour mash. Its intoxicating fumes overwhelming him, he welcomed the drunken stupor. He was discovered a week later on the eve of the festival, emaciated, drunk but happy. He was carried back to a fresh bed of banana leaves and left to sleep off his inebriation.

The shaman came to visit Bruno and burned and administered herbs, danced and prayed over his supine body. The chief sent a young maiden to massage his fever-wracked body and stroke his beard, which had turned as white as the peak of Mt. Oomoa.

During the course of Bruno's recovery the fates had visited Theonia and Makuto. Minuscule xylophagous insects attacked Theonia's bassoon, leaving only the metal parts behind, much like carnivores eating the flesh and leaving the bone.

This was not the end of Theonia's troubles. She fell ill with pleurisy and was unable to serenade Makuto, who had contracted elephantiasis, which in its early stages was a bonus for Theonia, increasing the size of Makuto's dork until it became too large and painful to use.

Bruno, witnessing their tribulations, felt vindicated. He overhauled his schooner and set sail on a cloudless day, a provident breeze filling his sails. He left behind a speechless Theonia and her lover, burdened by his own flesh.

Bruno plied the south seas selling Copra, lonely as the ancient mariner. Many a night alone in the coal black night he could hear Theonia's bassoon over the pitch of the waves and he laughed hysterically; and the sea birds knew he was mad.

The Unicorn

He was born back in some distant age, when the earth was just beginning to receive its creatures from the sea.

Contrary to tradition, he is not mythical, as most people are led to believe. He is very real, and roams the earth to this day.

His mother was a narwhal who lived in the frozen blue sea. She evolved over eons, one of many strange and beautiful compositions of nature. His father's spiraled ivory tusk was a gift of creation, passed on to his magical spawn.

She felt the tiny hoofs kicking in her womb and she knew she was about to give birth to a special offspring who was blessed by King Neptune.

In the stillness of the arctic dawn wastelands, amidst the majesty of towering icebergs, the Unicorn emerged from her body, as pure as the virgin ice and as unblemished as his surroundings. His white mane fluttered in the wind. The ivory tusk he inherited from his father was a creamy white, tipped with a sparkling jewel that glistened day and night.

Hungry wolves and polar bears came and sniffed his fragrant, newborn body and sensed he was sacred. They nuzzled him and brought him food. Seals, walruses and penguins huddled around him shielding him from the bitter wind.

A hunting party of Eskimos saw the congregation of animals and advanced with spears and clubs, ready to slaughter them for food and hides. Amazingly, the animals did not run away under attack. Instead, they formed an impenetrable circle to protect the Unicorn.

Some mysterious force stayed the hunters' hands. From within the circle, an aura of rainbow colors pulsated. The jewel from the Unicorn's tusk gave off a brilliant light that blinded the hunters. They dropped their weapons and fell to their knees in awe. The Unicorn glowed like the first evening star, a shimmering white radiance.

The protecting animal friends moved aside and the Unicorn emerged. Without hesitation or fear he approached each hunter and touched him with his jewelled tusk. The hunters were transformed by love. All their hunting instincts were subdued, their urge to kill gone. They threw their weapons into the sea and knelt in humility.

The Unicorn pranced quietly away with his admiring animal friends.

The Eskimos returned to their village humbled, spreading the legend of the Unicorn. From that day on they were more loving toward their wives and children and made peace with their enemies.

The Unicorn knew he had magical powers and he vowed to roam the earth with his message of love.

Word spread quickly. Many evil men plotted to kill him for his precious tusk and jewel.

But whenever they encountered him they fell back helpless. Good overcame evil. The greedy men felt their hearts swell. For the first time love filled their souls and they were transformed into innocent children.

The Unicorn wandered from Mesopotamia to Madagascar stopping wars, turning warlords, assassins and dictators into saviours.

Like love, the Unicorn will never die. He will forever seek out desperate men and heal them with his goodness.

Those of us who are in need of love and have love to give will find him and share his love. In our search for love, the Unicorn will find us.

Dedicated to my daughter, Josephine

Prose & Poetry

Autumn Thoughts

Maples standing like large bouquets, golden, amber and russet, radiating their brilliance in the rays of an early morning sun, dazzling in holy communion.

Leaves scurrying across the highway, pushed by a gentle wind, join their colorful companions in frolicking heaps. Fields of tawny grass undulating under a warm sun encourage petting, like a large friendly beast.

Mosaic patchworks of ploughed fields, unharvested cabbage sea-blue green, frosted pumpkins waiting to be pies or Jack-o-lanterns.

Woods and hedgerows, havens for wildlife, demarcations of nature's hand. The shimmering surface of ponds burnished by the sun, creating their last dance of seasonal joy before being frozen and stilled, waiting for the awakening kiss of spring.

Robins gone, hardy crested blue jays winging their ways in bright blue finery, defiant of the approaching winter.

Sweatered children with apple-red delicious cheeks gamboling in a mound of golden leaves, their shrieks and shouts a testimony to innocence shared with nature.

Goblins, witches and ghosts stir our ancestral imagination, a haunted house lingers in our mind, causing a pleasing shudder to reverberate through our mind and body.

Old people in the late autumn of their years, hobbled by life's adversity, others strong-willed and heroic, smiling and quick-witted, challenging the grim reaper.

Praise has been heaped by numerous poets better than I, but I must add mine to the glory of autumn and thanks for the beauty she bestows upon me.

A Rainbow Under the Stars

I was sitting in front of the fire in my cabin, looking into the leaping flames, unable to control my mesmerized mind as it leapt from fantasy to memories of exotic travels.

Recently having returned from Cuba, the torrid rhythms of Salsa and Afro/Cuban tempos still coursed through my veins, creating vivid impressions of undulating bodies, abandon, laughter and rum-scented breaths.

The weather here in Upstate New York was as unpredictable as a beautiful woman with many admirers.

Earlier we had a seasonal cold spell that only partially proved the Farmers Almanac forebodings. Meditatively puffing away on my recent acquisition of a Havana Romeo y Julieta Churchill cigar merely added to the pleasure and unreality of my present situation.

It had remained cold enough to produce a safe layer of ice, so I could do my first ice fishing. I caught pickerel, perch, small rainbow and brown trout on my tip-ups. My daughter, Josephine, was due to come home from boarding school for a temporary break, and I agreed to go and bring her home from Vermont.

The weather suddenly began to warm up, with the blame attributed from the El Niño current to celestial bombardments. The ice weakened rapidly as the snow melted, forming a pond upon the pond.

I continued to slosh out and mind my tip-ups on a respectable eight inches of ice. Several days of rain and continued balmy weather melted the remaining ice rapidly, but I bravely continued to fish.

Early one morning I saw my first coyote trudge forlornly over the sopping terrain, its long tail hanging listlessly, its pointed muzzle jutting forward as it ambled indifferently.

It was time to gather up Josephine, so I decided to leave my tip-ups out, knowing I would return the following day. The expected return of cold weather did not happen, and it also brought on a severe case of the flu. When I returned early evening the following day, I was quite ill and my tip-ups were sitting in several inches of water. I had no interest in retrieving them.

I got weaker and so did the ice. I thought of going out in my boat as a safety measure, pushing it in front of me, but I had neither the strength nor the inclination. When I felt my strength return the ice around the shore had melted. I walked to the end of the dock and stepped on the ice. There was a rubbery response and the ice cracked. I leapt back on the dock. Of the five tip-ups, four flags were up, indicating strikes. It was frustrating, but prudence, which has not always been one of my mainstays, prevailed.

Over the course of several more warm days I watched my tip-ups sink like flagships under fire. The ice melted and we were back to water once again.

While I was in Cuba the weather reverted to our traditional Upstate winter and new ice formed. I had five old wooden tip-ups left and put them to good use. With my gas-powered auger I was back in business, all within binocular view from my back porch.

The fishing was slow. Some surveyor friends set up a chain of tip-ups. They lost some big fish but presented me with two pickerel and two jack perch.

After another warm day of fishing the temperature dropped suddenly at night to 5 degrees F. When I finished my dinner — a cup of espresso and a Montecristo Cuban cigar — I headed out on the ice.

The sky was flooded with stars, the air sharp and clear. My

flashlight beam reflected off the frozen surface. My afternoon footprints in the wet snow were frozen, so they looked like Neil Armstrong's from the lunar landing. One small red flag was up, bobbing gently in a stiff cold breeze. When I lifted up the tip-up I noticed all the line on the spool had run off and my hopes were high.

As I pulled in nearly seventy-five feet of line with weeds attached, there was suddenly a heavy and reluctant tug at the other end, and I knew it was a big fish.

It pulled the line through my fingers as it went on a desperate run to escape. Each time I got it near the hole it would take off and I couldn't get a look at it. I was afraid the line would be cut on the sharp edge of the ice. After several more runs it tired and I coaxed it up with a steady pull. Out of the hole appeared a silvery speckled head and I gasped and laughed at the huge size, already boasting mentally to my friends. He was too proud to accept my derisive laughter and overconfidence, though; he gave a sudden lunge and twist, broke off the hook, and slid back down into the hole before I had the sense to grab him.

My rainbow under the stars outwitted me as I knelt as if in prayer, shivering, feeling proud that we had met and he had regained his freedom.

March 1995
Leland Pond, New York

The Cabin

The wind blew hard out of the northeast, scudding gray-flecked dirty, billowing masses of vaporish clouds into herds. Lorne had come down to the cabin to fish, but was trapped by the deluge that had been threatening all morning.

The cabin had a musty, mildewed odor that was not pleasant. Magazines, their corners chewed by winter's mice, lay scattered and forlorn on an end table. Dust had settled everywhere, providing a microscopic accumlation of careless time. Faces in photographs retreated further into the past, dimmed by the smoke of many fires.

The iron stove looked cold and lifeless, its doors open gaping like someone gulping their last breath. The windowpane was cracked and water oozed and followed the jagged line like a meandering river. Rosaries of rain beaded under the sill to form a litany of silver-threaded pencil streams that drilled a monotonous tattoo on the porch planks.

At the pond's edge a red-winged blackbird clung to the end of a cattail and seemed to enjoy its precarious position as the reed bent and sprung under its weight. A muskrat knifed its way across the pond, its delicate whiskers aloof, creating a neat wedge in its wake.

Lorne shivered slightly and felt very alone. Delicate patterns of miraculously constructed cobwebs were highlighted in the gloom of the cabin corners. The cabin belonged to encroach

162

ing time and the insects and animals who lived there; Lorne felt like an intruder.

For the moment his own life felt meaningless and he imagined his body decaying and crumbling, becoming mummified — being discovered by some curious archaeologist.

The steady dripping of the rain mesmerized him. He stared as if drugged at his fishing poles and tackle box near the door where he had left them. He had not removed his yellow rain suit, but even the bright color could not cheer him up.

A large, ratty, overstuffed chair beckoned. Its dingy plaid fabric gave up a cloud of dust when he slouched down into it and the coiled springs dug into his bottom.

The day's ruined fishing didn't matter anymore. He was sinking into a helpless depression. All of the bad moments of his life swirled around him and he fought them off as best he could in this vulnerable state.

The room got darker. A sudden flash of lightning penetrated the darkness, illuminating the dreary surroundings and his soul. Seconds later it was followed by a loud clap of thunder, which shook the cabin and reverberated through his body. Lorne couldn't move. The ozone penetrated his nostrils and the hair bristled on the nape of his neck. He curled himself up into a tight ball like some sleeping animal, closed his eyes and could feel the hot, moist vapor of his labored breathing.

He felt warm, a ray of sun poured through the grimy window and fell across his outstretched legs. A large moth was beating its wings against the window.

A bad dream of drowning in a car was just receding from his memory and the desperate moth gave him a sudden feeling of how precious life is. He opened the door and shooed it out.

He looked at his watch. He had slept for several hours, and felt it was another day or another life.

He walked outside into the sunlight. The wildflowers were bright and cheerful and there was bird song. The leaves moved gently in a soft, warm breeze and the fear slowly left him. Lorne sat down by the bank of the pond in the wet grass. A leopard frog leapt into the water.

He sat for a long time, until he felt sure of his emotions. He got into his pickup truck and started for home, a few miles away. He remembered he left his fishing tackle, but he didn't want to go back. He told himself he would go back tomorrow.

When he arrived home his wife Cleo, was canning tomatoes in the kitchen. Her face was red and sweaty. She asked disinterestedly how the fishing was. Lorne answered, "They weren't biting," and went into the living room. And poured himself three fingers of scotch.

A Rainy Day

Bill woke up several times during the night at the cottage. It was mid-July, and being on the lake there was a persistent dampness, but strangely, no night sounds.

The old refrigerator had a life of its own. It would kick on for a short cycle, like a June bug gives a few desperate gasps, vibrate fitfully, and stops suddenly with a death rattle.

The stillness and darkness were not threatening. He had a new love to refer to who brought him warmth and comfort. It was a year and a half since his separation, with a costly divorce in progress. There were no regrets, but painful memories worked their ways through the uncaulked seams of his mind. He was learning to live again after twenty-three years, and like a child taking its first steps, each day added strength and confidence.

Bill tried not to look at the clock, remembering the advice of some sleep therapist, but he couldn't help himself. It was still dark outside. He listened intently, hearing no wind or rain; just a persistent vacuum. The electric blanket, set on number four, glowed and took the chill out of the bed — no substitute for his lover's body, but welcome in the ebony emptiness.

He thought of a friend he had called earlier that night, someone from his boyhood who was a year older and concerned about prostate cancer. Another longtime friend his age told him his 35-year-old son was killed on a construction job. They had not been close, which made the loss seem even more tormenting.

165

The obituaries are full of 69-year-old men succumbing to the tally of life's adversities, and Bill was fully aware of the precious moments left to him. Rarely did he dwell on the subject of death. His health was good, he had many interests, and his new relationship added to his vigor. Each day was a prize and a surprise, and he let the gift unwrap itself.

Thinking of these complexities, he drifted back to a restless sleep and woke to the gentle drizzle of rain on the screened-in porch outside his bedroom window. It was not easy to push the covers aside and leave the secure warmth of his bed, but with a supreme effort he swung his legs over the bed's edge.

Bill liked the first morning rituals, hearing the early morning news, the fresh smell of coffee, squeezing a couple of oranges, toast with good jam. It all had a powerful, simple meaning.

His new girlfriend, Linda, pervaded all his thoughts so that each chore turned into a pleasant task. Being retired he set his own pace. Feed the birds, check the fishing lines, make out a shopping list. Don't look too far ahead, let the day unfold like a flower with the first touch of the morning sun.

The rain persisted at a warm, windless pace, falling straight down with the drops seeming to connect. Bill felt mildly restless, but the fertile smell of the earth quickly distracted him. The birds were gladdened by the rain and fought for positions at the feeder. A gray squirrel waited patiently below for the droppings.

Bill left the house, unmindful of his jacket, and climbed into his new van. The engine turned over quietly, the windshield wipers gliding back and forth, squeezing the rain from the glass. He took a gulp of hot coffee from his mug and thought of fresh strawberries, the first string beans, peas, and most of all Linda. This already was a special day.

Half Witicisms

Half-Witicisms

"A bachelor does not know the joy of argument."

"My son, I will dispense advice generously but please do not ask for money."

"Like love the fire first warms the toes then the heart."

"She said it with a smile in her voice."

"A little booze a little snooze."

"Indolence makes the heart beat slower."

"Politially correct but at times inacurate"

"If you decide to become a fiction writer I suggest you develop your own character first."

"I am happy to give advice and be rid of it."

"What's all the talk about sex? Lets do it!"

"The leaves of life keep falling on my head and I have not yet reached the autumn of my years."

"The things that I wanted so badly yesterday I don't need today."

Danger falling stock zone!

I flogged a bishop, spanked a nun, holy Jesus I'm having fun.

He kicked the bottle, he kicked his wife now he leads a merry life.

Give Me Puberty or Give Me Death

My wife and I had great oral sex, we shared the same toothbrush.

A cold front is moving in, must be my ex-wives.

My dog gives me more love than my wife and more loyalty than my mistress.

Couples copulating in Copely Square
Sparks flying from their pubic hair
Unmindful of the cold night air

Danger, falling angel zone

The midget was a capillary boar

Womyn who are politically correct make it difficult for a man to become erect

Souls rebuilt and spirits rekindled

I make my living as a writer. Can't you tell? I have no shoes

With all my faults I love me still

Time will tell, spare the gossips